Best
TEA SHOP WALKS
in the
CLWYDIAN HILLS
& WELSH BORDERLANDS

Dorothy Hamilton

Published by Sigma Leisure – an imprint of
Sigma Press, 1 South Oak Lane, Wilmslow, Cheshire SK9 6AR, England.

British Library Cataloguing in Publication Data
A CIP record for this book is available from the British Library.

ISBN: 1-85058-727-2

Typesetting and Design by: Sigma Press, Wilmslow, Cheshire.

Cover: Castell Dinas Bran from the Panorama Walk *(Dorothy Hamilton)*; Cover design by MFP Design & Print

Maps: location map – Morag Perrott; sketch maps – Jeremy Semmens

Photographs: Dorothy Hamilton

Printed by: MFP Design & Print

Contents

The Walks

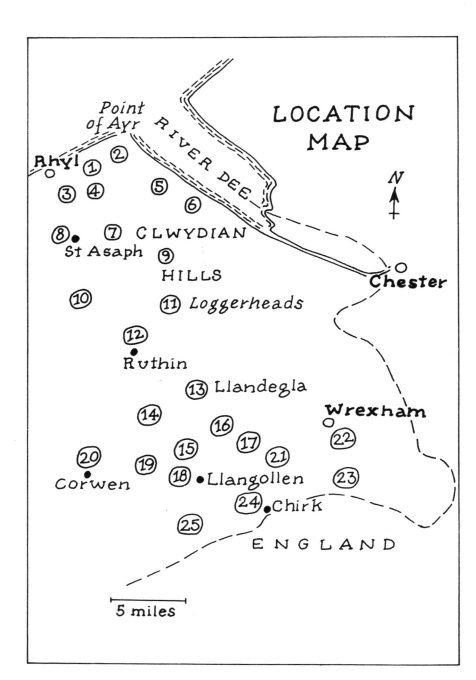

LOCATION
MAP

Point of Ayr

RIVER DEE

Rhyl ① ②
③ ④ ⑤
⑥
⑧ ⑦ CLWYDIAN
St Asaph ⑨
HILLS
⑩ ⑪ Loggerheads
⑫
Ruthin
⑬ Llandegla
⑭
⑯ Wrexham
⑮ ⑰ ㉒
⑳ ⑲ ㉑
⑱ Llangollen ㉓
Corwen
㉔ Chirk
㉕
ENGLAND

Chester

N

5 miles

Introduction

The Clwydian hills and Welsh borderlands comprise a beautiful area rich in variety and historical interest. Surprisingly, many walkers have not yet discovered this fascinating part of North Wales.

An Area of Outstanding Natural Beauty, the Clwydian range extends inland from the sea and offers wonderful walking over limestone hills, through woodlands and across heather moorland. The Offa's Dyke long distance trail traverses the range and crosses the highest peak, Moel Famau, at 1820 feet. Iron Age forts occupy some of the hilltops.

To the west of the range lies the peaceful, lush green Vale of Clwyd with its riverside walks, cathedral and medieval castles. For hundreds of years the valley was a battleground between the Welsh kingdoms of Gwynedd and Powys and, later, between the princes of Gwynedd and the Norman invaders.

Splendid walks may be found farther south on the heather-clad Llantysilio Mountain and from the spectacular Horseshoe Pass. The limestone cliffs of the Eglwyseg escarpment are prominent on several routes north of Llangollen. Fine walks start from the Dee valley, climbing to hilltops with historic remains, or following the riverbank and the delightful Llangollen canal. The tranquil valley of Glyn Ceiriog marks the southern boundary of the area covered in this guide.

To fully appreciate this part of north Wales, it is helpful to know a little of its history. People have been living in the area since prehistoric times. The first evidence of people being in Wales comes from the Pontnewydd cave near St Asaph. It overlooks the Elwy river on the west side of the Vale of Clwyd. They were of the Neanderthal type, living about 200,000 BC, and hunted wolf, bear, leopard, rhinoceros and bison. Remains of three people including human teeth, hand axes and scrapers were discovered. The Cae Gwyn and Ffynnon Beuno caves, in use about 30,000 BC, are seen on the walk from Tremeirchion. Bones of Neolithic people were found in the Gop caves near Trelawnyd.

The summits of the Clwydian range may have formed a trade route during the Bronze Age. Several burial mounds of this period are in the vicinity of Gop hill and on the Eglwyseg plateau above Llangollen. Dating about 1500 BC, a patterned gold cape, made from beaten gold and lined with cloth, has been found at Mold. It was in a stone chamber under a mound and with it were amber beads and human bones.

Celtic people arrived in Britain about 500 BC and they built the Iron Age hill forts on the Clwydian hills. Excavations of the sites have revealed little about their way of life and few hut circles. The Deceangli tribe inhabited this part of north Wales and they may have practised transhumance by living in lowland settlements most of the year and making use of the hills as pasture during the summer months.

Although the Romans conquered Wales, they do not appear to have built forts in this area. They exploited the mineral wealth and mined lead near Prestatyn. For many centuries after the Romans left Britain, the Welsh borderlands were a battleground. However, the pagan Angles and Saxons did not penetrate north Wales, and this allowed Christianity to flourish. Kentigern founded a religious centre at St Asaph, and a large monastery was established at Bangor is y Coed (Bangor on Dee). In a great battle during the early years of the 7th century, King Ethelfrith of Northumbria destroyed the monastery. The monks who escaped slaughter fled to Bardsey Island, off the Lleyn peninsula.

In the 8th century, King Offa of Mercia built his great earthwork as a defence against the Welsh. Another dyke, Wat's Dyke was built a few miles farther east about the same period. Although no evidence has been left of any settlements, Viking invaders ravaged the coast of north Wales until crushed by Rhodri Mawr, ruler of Gwynedd and Powys.

For short periods in the following centuries, Wales was united as one country. First by Hywel Dda in the 10th century, and later by Gruffudd ap Llywelyn who inherited Gwynedd and Powys and won Deheubarth and Morgannwg. By this time, the English had encroached across the border; Gruffudd drove them out and occupied the stronghold on Twt hill at Rhuddlan. The Norman Earl Robert later built a castle on this site and battles continued between the Welsh rulers and Normans. Owain Gwynedd built his castle at Llandegla. In 1267, Llywelyn ap Gruffudd was recognised by Henry III as Prince of Wales. Conflict between Edward I and Llywelyn's brother Dafydd triggered the king's campaign, which led to the English conquest of Wales.

Edward I constructed new castles and English colonists occupied his fortified towns. They had more privileges than the Welsh and at first their presence was resented. In the year 1400 Owain Glyndwr led his unsuccessful rebellion against English rule and burnt towns in the Vale of Clwyd. The war was to last ten years. Unrest followed in the Wars of the Roses and peace did not finally come to the area until Henry Tudor gained the throne in 1485. The Acts of Union in 1536 and 1543 united Wales politically with England.

The Tea Shops

Ending a walk at a tearoom for a light meal completes the enjoyment of a day spent in the beautiful Welsh countryside. All the teashops welcome walkers, but please be considerate and remove wet waterproofs, and clean or remove muddy boots.

The establishments chosen are varied and include farmhouses, a former mill, a castle, a garden centre and a building that was once a workhouse. Most tearooms provide home cooking, especially home-made cakes. Approximately half of them are open all year. The majority would appreciate advance notice of the arrival of a large walking group.

The Walks

Apart from one walk between stations on the Llangollen Railway, all the walks in this guide are circular. They range between 3 and 10 miles, from leisurely strolls suitable for families, to routes for those who enjoy more strenuous hikes. A few follow level paths but most require some climbing.

The walks explore a wide variety of countryside from towpaths and riverbanks to woodland and heather covered hills. Boots are not essential on most of the walks but they are recommended for the higher walks in the Clwydian hills, Llantysilio Mountain and crossing the Eglwyseg screes. They add comfort by giving security to the ankles and keep the feet dry in wet and muddy conditions. Warm clothing, including head covering and gloves, are essential for the longer and/or higher routes in the winter. Waterproofs should be carried if there is any possibility of rain. Drinks, hot or cold accord-

ing to preference and the season, and a snack such as fruit or a chocolate bar, add enjoyment to the longer walks.

The directions and maps in this guidebook should be all you need
to complete the walks. Ordnance Survey maps would help you to
identify the hills around you, and places not mentioned in the text.
They are essential if you wish to make any changes to the routes. The
maps referred to are the Landranger series (1:50 000) and the Pathfinder series (1:25 000). New Explorer maps, which give better value
for money, are gradually replacing the Pathfinders.

The Offa's Dyke Path

Eleven walks in this guide follow sections of the Offa's Dyke Path.
This 177-mile route stretches from Chepstow on the River Severn to
Prestatyn on the North Wales Coast. Its name stems from the dyke
constructed as a boundary marker by King Offa of Mercia in the 8th
century. The long distance route follows the line of the dyke from
Chepstow to the River Dee. It then veers slightly west to traverse the
Clwydian hills, whilst the dyke runs north to end at Treuddyn near
Mold. Stretches of the dyke can be seen on Walks 21 and 24.

The northern section of the long distance path passes through superb, varied scenery and countryside, ranging from the towpath
across the Pontcysyllte Aqueduct to the Eglwyseg screes and the
highest summit on the Clwydian range, all of which feature on walks
in this book.

Public Transport

Almost all the walks are accessible by public transport. Details are
given for each walk. Free bus timetables are available at information
centres.

Useful Phone Numbers

Arriva Buses (Rhyl area): 01745 343721

Busline (Wrexham): 01978 266166

Llangollen Tourist Information Centre: 01978 860828

Prestatyn Information Centre: 01745 889092

Rhyl Tourist Information Centre: 01745 344515

Wrexham Tourist Information Centre: 01978 292015

Welsh Place Names

Place names in Wales can cause problems. Learning these pronunciations will help.

A	=	ah
C	=	k (hard)
Dd	=	'th' as in 'the'
E	=	eh
F	=	v
G	=	as in 'go'
I	=	ee
Ll	=	say 'l', hold tongue in this position and blow gently
O	=	oh
Th	=	as in 'through'
W	=	usually as in oo ('cwm' sounds like 'coom')
Y	=	as e in 'the'

A few translations will aid understanding of place names. The following words are used frequently:

Aber	=	estuary, river mouth
Afon	=	river
Allt	=	slope
Bach/fach	=	small
Bedd	=	grave
Blaen	=	head of valley
Bont/pont	=	bridge
Bryn	=	hill
Bwlch	=	pass
Cae	=	field
Caer	=	fort
Canol	=	middle, centre
Capel	=	chapel
Castell	=	castle
Cefn	=	ridge
Ceunant	=	gorge
Clogwyn	=	precipice
Coch	=	red
Coed	=	woodland
Cors/gors	=	bog, marsh
Craig	=	crag
Croes	=	cross
Cwm	=	valley
Dinas	=	fort
Dol/ddol	=	meadow

Drws	=	door
Du/ddu	=	black
Dwr	=	water
Dyffryn	=	valley
Eglwys	=	church
Ffordd	=	road
Ffridd	=	mountain pasture
Fynnon	=	well, spring
Garth	=	enclosure
Glan	=	riverbank
Glas	=	blue, green
Gwaun/waun	=	moor
Gwyn	=	white
Gwynt	=	wind
Hafod/hafodty	=	summer dwelling
Hen	=	old
Hendre	=	winter dwelling
Isaf	=	below
Llan	=	church
Llethr	=	slope
Llety	=	lodging, inn
Llwyd	=	grey
Llyn	=	lake
Maen	=	stone
Maes	=	field
Mawr/fawr	=	big
Melin/felin	=	mill
Moel/foel	=	hill
Morfa	=	marsh
Mynydd/fynydd	=	mountain
Nant	=	stream
Newydd	=	new
Ogof	=	cave
Pandy	=	fulling mill
Pant	=	hollow
Parc	=	park, field
Pen	=	head, top
Pentre	=	village
Pistyll	=	spout, cataract
Plas	=	mansion
Pwll	=	pool
Rhaeadr	=	waterfall
Rhiw	=	hill
Rhos	=	moorland

Rhyd	=	ford
Sarn	=	causeway, road
Siglen	=	bog, swamp
Tan	=	under
Tir	=	land
Tomen	=	mound
Traeth	=	beach
Traws	=	across
Tref	=	town
Trwyn	=	promontory
Twr	=	tower
Ty	=	house
Tyddyn	=	small farm
Uchaf	=	upper
Y/yr	=	the
Yn	=	in
Ysgubor	=	barn
Ystrad	=	valley floor

1. Prestatyn

Route: This superb walk follows a spectacular short section of the Offa's Dyke Path before climbing to above Gwaenysgor village. The long steady climb is rewarded with lovely views of the surrounding countryside. Care must be taken on the escarpment, especially in windy weather. A section of path may be muddy after heavy rain.

Distance: 4 miles.

How to get there: Prestatyn is on the A548 coast road, east of Rhyl.

Public Transport: Trains to Prestatyn. Buses from Rhyl and Chester.

Start: GR 068828. Car park off Nant Hall Road, near the bottom of the High Street.

Maps: OS Landranger 116 or Pathfinder 737.

Prestatyn's history dates from prehistoric times. In 1924, a skeleton believed to be Neolithic, the 'Prestatyn Lady', was found beneath the High Street. On the south side of the town, there is a small Roman bathhouse and it is thought the Romans worked lead or silver mines nearby. The Normans built a motte and bailey castle on the coastal plain east of the present town. A few years later the Welsh, under Owain Gwynedd, destroyed it. Although lead mining was a major industry here in the mid-18th century, the population in 1811 was only 178. The settlement consisted of a few miners' and quarrymen's cottages. The coming of the railway made little impact at first and the town did not grow substantially until the beginning of the 20th century, when estates were sold for development.

The Tea Shop

Eva's Pantry is located at the bottom of the High Street close to the junction with Nant Hall Road. The varied menu includes main meals with traditional puddings, soups, sandwiches, toasties, pancakes and home-made cakes and pastries. Open all year Monday to Saturday 9.00am-4.30pm. Tel: 01745 857484.

The Walk

1. From the car park, walk out to the High Street and turn left up-hill. At the top of the hill cross to a road called Fforddlas, which is to the left of the Cross Foxes. Follow the road uphill, and continue along it when it bears right and becomes Bishopswood Road. Take the first road left and pass the Prestatyn Hillside car park.

2. Bear left with the road and, shortly, turn right on a footpath to follow the Offa's Dyke Path. The path climbs gently above a quarry. Climb some wooden steps and follow a fence on the left.

    From the limestone escarpment, views extend along the coast to the Great Orme. In summer wild thyme and the common rockrose may be seen growing near the path. On the lower slopes of the hill, in Bishopswood, the Fish Mine was worked for lead and calcite until the end of the 19th century. The name is derived from the shape of the waste tip, which was thought to resemble a plaice.

Gwaenysgor Church

3. The path descends slightly. When the path reaches the start of a steep descent, turn left over a stile to leave the Offa's Dyke Path. Follow the right-hand boundary of a field and continue ahead through trees and gorse. Cross a stile and follow an enclosed footpath. Pass a grilled well on the right and continue on an access lane to a road. Turn right for approximately 100 metres to a lane junction. The walk turns left here, but you may like to see Gwaenysgor village and church before continuing on the walk.

    The Church of St Mary Magdalene dates from the 13th century. There is a 14th-century lepers' window and this allowed the sufferers to see the service from outside the church. The church also has a devil's door, which was for the re-admittance of those who had been excommunicated and repented. The parish is well known for its parish registers, which are unbroken from the time of Henry VIII.

4. Continuing on the walk, follow the quiet lane gently uphill. Over to your right is the wooded Gop Hill.
    •
    On the top of Gop Hill are the remains of the largest cairn in Wales. Archaeological excavations revealed only animal bones, but caves which contained Neolithic human remains lie on the south side of the hill. According to legend, the cairn is the burial place of Boudicca, Queen of the Iceni. Ghosts of Roman soldiers have been seen in the field below the cairn.

5. Ignore a track on the left and pass the drive to Teila Farm on the right. There are soon views of the Dee estuary. When the lane becomes rougher, continue ahead and ignore a stile on the left next to a gate. In another 200 metres, at the start of a descent, cross a stile on the left.

6. Cross the field half-left to a stile that is to the right of a mast and left of a gate. From this point there are great views of the coastline. Walk downhill, slanting left to a stile in a fence that descends from the mast buildings. Cross the next field by walking directly ahead to a stile in the right corner. Descend the field to reach a fence and turn left to walk beside it. Cross a stile in the bottom corner of the field and bear right to a stile near woodland. Descend steps and follow a clear path downhill to a lane.

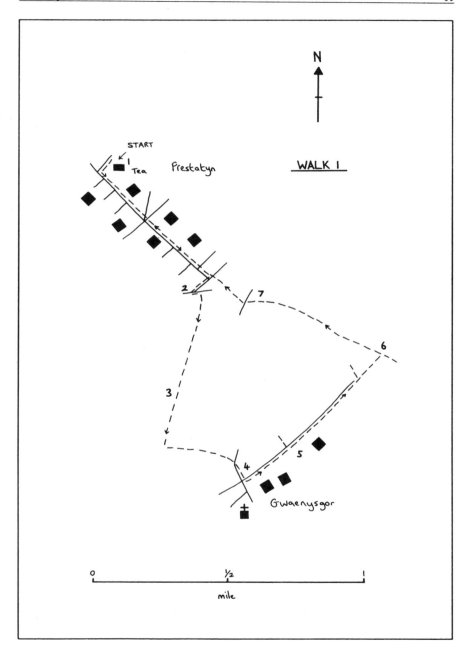

7. Turn left uphill on the lane and, before a left bend, turn right on a path. Descend through woodland. Cross a drive and track. Take a path through bushes and continue downhill until you join the lane again near an observatory. Bear left and, shortly, take another path downhill to emerge on a road. Turn left and almost immediately right to retrace your steps along Fforddlas Road. Descend the High Street to the car park and Eva's Pantry.

2. Gronant

Route: This is a lovely short walk through peaceful countryside. Ascending tracks and paths lead onto a hillside with superb views of the coast and Dee estuary.

Distance: 4 miles.

How to get there: Gronant is on the A548, east of Prestatyn. At the crossroads in Gronant, take the road signed Presthaven and Lower Gronant to the car park.

Public Transport: Buses from Rhyl and Chester. The nearest railway station is at Prestatyn.

Start: GR 091837. Car park in Shore Road, opposite the Crofter's Pantry.

Maps: OS Landranger 116 or OS Pathfinder 737.

The Tea Shop

The Crofter's Pantry in Shore Road offers a large selection of sandwiches, toasties and cakes. There are outside tables, as well as inside, and food can be bought to take away. Gifts are also on sale. Open 1 March to 30 September every day. In the high season (end June-mid September) 9.00am-5.00pm. In the low season 9.00am-3.00pm. Sometimes open in October, phone to check beforehand. Tel: 01745 856075.

The Walk

1. From the car park turn right and continue ahead to the A548. Turn left and almost immediately turn right on a road signposted Upper Gronant. Follow the road uphill and turn left at the top in the direction of Llanasa. In 300 metres, where the gradient eases, turn right along Pentre Lane.

2. Pass the old school on the right and, shortly, bear right at a bridleway sign. Walk uphill on a shady track and pass an old quarry below on the left. Farther on, ignore a stile on the left.

    As the track rises there are magnificent views north-east to the Point of Ayr lighthouse, Dee estuary, Hilbre Islands and the Wirral. Trinity House built the lighthouse in 1776-1777 and it showed two lights, one towards the Great Orme and the other towards the Wirral. After the Dee lightship was established in 1883, the lighthouse closed down. The Point of Ayr is an important nature reserve for birds overwintering or resting whilst on migration. Waders roost and feed on the mudflats whilst the marsh attracts wildfowl.

3.   Continue uphill. The track descends slightly to give a wide view of the rolling, wooded Flintshire countryside. When you reach a junction of tracks, turn right on a bridleway. As you walk uphill, stop occasionally to enjoy backward views. Pass a drive to a house on the right. Continue on the track, which dwindles to a narrow path. It is bordered by wild flowers in spring and early summer. Pass a ruin on the right and, in another 350 metres, pass a pool on the left which is hidden behind trees.

4.   In approximately 50 metres cross a stile on the right and walk directly ahead towards the sea. Pass some gorse on the left and descend with a fence on your right. There are fine views towards the sea, Point of Ayr lighthouse, Dee estuary and the Wirral.

View from the hillside above Gronant

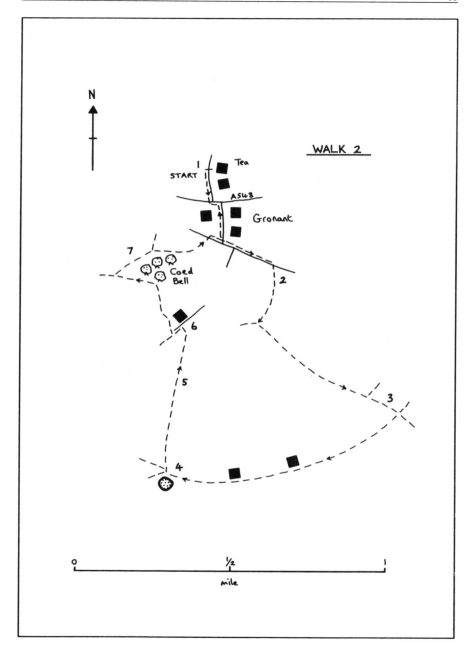

5. Go through an old kissing gate and walk downhill to the right-hand corner of a wood. After going through a field gate, follow the fence on your left until you reach a stile. Walk ahead in the direction of a farm roof. Cross a stile and descend to a lane.

6. Turn left and in approximately 30 metres cross a stile on the right. Follow the right-hand fence to another stile and continue beside a fence on the right. Cross a ladder stile and follow a fairly level path through the wood. Cross a stile and walk ahead slightly above a fence. When you reach a fence corner, turn right and follow the left-hand fence to a stile. Cross the field ahead to a stile at the edge of Coed Bell Wood.

7. Descend a clear path to the bottom of the wood. Ignore a stile on the left and follow the edge of the trees to a kissing gate. Walk diagonally right to a kissing gate in the bottom right-hand corner of the field. Turn right along the road and in 50 metres bear left downhill to retrace your steps to the car park and Crofter's Pantry.

3. Rhuddlan

Route: An easy completely flat walk on dykes and paths around the Clwyd estuary. The route follows a section of the North Wales Path and is good for bird watching.

Distance: 5½ miles.

How to get there: Rhuddlan is south of Rhyl on the A525 and A547.

Public Transport: Buses from Rhyl, Prestatyn and Ruthin. Trains to Rhyl.

Start: GR 024779. Rhuddlan Castle.

Maps: OS Landranger 116 or OS Pathfinders 737 and 755 .

Rhuddlan takes its name from the 'red bank' on the eastern bank of the River Clwyd. The site was strategically important because it overlooked the ford nearest the sea and there was no other crossing

The Vale of Clwyd from Twt Hill

for several miles. The ford was directly below Twt hill, a Norman motte 300 metres upstream of the castle.

The English are said to have won a battle at Rhuddlan in 796, the year King Offa of Mercia died. About 100 years later the Welsh regained the area and in 1016 the local chieftain, Llywelyn ap Seisyllt, built a castle at Rhuddlan, possibly on Twt hill. Gruffudd ap Llywelyn used it as a base for raids into England and in 1063 it was destroyed by Earl Harold. Ten years later the Norman lord Robert of Rhuddlan, a cousin of Hugh Avranches the Earl of Chester, built a motte and bailey castle on Twt hill. It stood 60 feet above the river and was protected by a valley and ditch. He founded a borough, which had a mint, a church, a mill and 18 burgesses.

Owain Gwynedd captured Rhuddlan in 1150, but it was taken by the English seven years later. In 1167 he recaptured the castle and it was held almost continuously by the Welsh until 1241, when it was taken by Henry III. Llywelyn ap Gruffudd was recognised as Prince of Wales by the king. However, Llywelyn refused to pay homage to the succeeding king, Henry III's son Edward I. Edward took the castle in 1277 and work was started on the stone castle and a new town.

The first work on the castle was by Master Bertram, but after a few months it was taken over by the famous architect of Edward I's castles, James of St George. The castle was positioned so that it could be supplied by sea and the River Clwyd was diverted from its meandering course into a deep-water channel that follows a straight line to the sea. It took over 70 men three years to do the work. The river is tidal to just above Rhuddlan.

Owain Glyndwr burnt the town in 1400 but failed to take the castle. During the Civil War the castle was held for the king until 1646 when it was surrendered to the Parliamentarians. Two years later it was partly demolished.

The street pattern in the centre of modern Rhuddlan is much the same as Edward I's original design. Parliament House is thought to have been the courthouse. The castle is open every day May-September from 10.00am-5.00pm (charge). A path from the castle can be followed to Twt hill. If the castle is closed, or not visited, Twt hill can be reached by a footpath from the lane.

The Tea Shop

Ye Olde Castle Tea Shoppe is located directly opposite the castle entrance. Lunches and afternoon teas are served. There is a delicious selection of home-made cakes, including coffee cake, apple pie and bara brith. Open all year, seven days a week. Hours are 10.00am-4.30pm April to September. Between October and March the tea shop closes at 4.00pm. Tel: 01745 591190.

The Walk

1. With your back to the castle, turn left to walk down Castle Street. On reaching the main road, bear left and cross the River Clwyd. In 150 metres, after passing The Marsh Warden, turn right along Marsh Road.

2. Pass under the A525 and pass a caravan park. At the end of the road, cross a stile and continue on a track alongside marshes and the River Clwyd.

   The Clwyd estuary attracts many waders and wildfowl. Birds likely to be seen include shelduck, wigeon, oystercatcher, dunlin, curlew and redshank.

3. After crossing the River Gele, continue on an embankment. Shortly before reaching the railway line, cross a stile and follow the track to a lane. Turn right to pass under the railway and continue ahead to the Foryd Bridge. Turn right to cross the bridge in the direction of Rhyl.

   You are now on the North Wales Path, a long distance route between Bangor and Prestatyn. The Foryd Bridge was built in 1930 to replace a toll bridge. Before the coming of the railway most visitors to Rhyl arrived by boat. Paddle steamers made regular trips between Liverpool and Rhyl and the journey took about three hours each way. Until 1800 Rhyl had only existed as an area of marsh within the parish of Rhuddlan. Realising the site, with its nearby sands, had potential as a resort, some land-owners drained an area of marshland and put it up for sale as small plots. The population grew slowly until the Rhyl Improvement Act in 1852 gave a spurt to development. By 1861 the population was almost 3000. A pier was opened six years later and Rhyl became a typical Victorian re-sort with arcades, side-shows and winter gardens. Since the 1960s, although Rhyl has many modern attractions for family visitors, its popularity as a resort has declined.

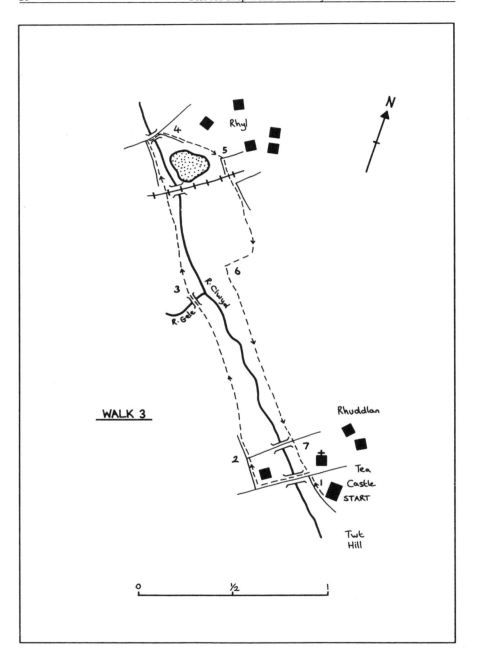

N

Rhyl

4

5

R. Clwyd

3

R. Gele

6

WALK 3

Rhuddlan

2   7

Tea
Castle
START

Twt
Hill

0   ½   1

4. On the east side of the bridge, the road divides. Take the right fork and, in a few metres, veer right onto the tarmac path alongside the Marine Lake. Turn left and follow the path to the Sea Cadets' Boathouse.

   The Marine Lake has been created on land that was previously a salt marsh. It covers 40 acres and, in winter, ducks and swans may be seen here. It opened in 1895 as a pleasure park and ornamental lake.

5. After passing the boathouse, bear left to follow an access road to a crossroads. Turn right along Westbourne Avenue and at its end, cross a footbridge over the railway. Walk ahead and cross Marsh Road to another road. Continue to the end of this road and cross a stile on the right. Follow the path as it bears left, parallel to a fence and caravan site. The path leads to a stile near the fence. Continue along an embankment with a high fence on the right and the caravan site on the left. Ignore a footpath on the left and follow the embankment to the River Clwyd.

6. Continue along the dyke with the river on your right. Cross a few stiles and go under the A525. Pass St Mary's Church on your left.

   The Church of St Mary was founded about 1300 and 200 years later it was given a second nave and a tower. Inside there are some 13th and 14th-century monuments. The church is open to visitors during the summer months on Thursday afternoons.

7. Descend the embankment and follow a track to the main road. Turn left into Rhuddlan and return to your starting place at the castle. To visit Twt hill by public footpath, bear right on a lane to have the castle on your right. In a few metres turn right on a track signposted Twt hill and St Asaph. On emerging in a field, walk ahead to a stile and ascend Twt hill. From the mound there are fine views of the Vale of Clwyd.

4. Dyserth

Route: A varied walk through fields and woodland to a superb viewpoint overlooking the Vale of Clwyd. The route continues on a section of the Offa's Dyke Path before descending to the pretty village of Cwm. Uphill sections are short.

Distance: 6 miles.

How to get there: Take the A5151 to Dyserth and follow the signs to the waterfall.

Public Transport: Buses from Rhyl and Prestatyn.

Start: GR 056793. Car park near the waterfall.

Maps: OS Landranger 116 or Pathfinders 737 and 755.

Dyserth is well known for its attractive waterfall which plummets 60 feet over a limestone rock. There is a small entrance fee to view the fall. The church of St Bridget and St Cwyfaen has a medieval stained glass window. Henry III built a castle on a hill south of Graig Fawr in 1241 and 22 years later it was destroyed by Llywelyn ap Gruffudd.

The Tea Shop

Situated at the entrance to the falls, The Waterfalls Café provides tables outside near the stream. It used to be the village sweet shop. Hot snacks and afternoon teas are served. Open Easter to September. Usual hours are 9.00am-5.00pm. On wet days the café may close much earlier.

The Walk

1.   From the car park turn left and pass the waterfall entrance and café on the left. In a few metres turn left between the shop and a house. Bear right up steps and ignore other paths on the right. On reaching a lane, turn left downhill on a path and cross a foot-bridge over the River Ffyddion. Follow a level path through the trees. Now dry, the path is an old leat which carried water to the mines at Meliden.

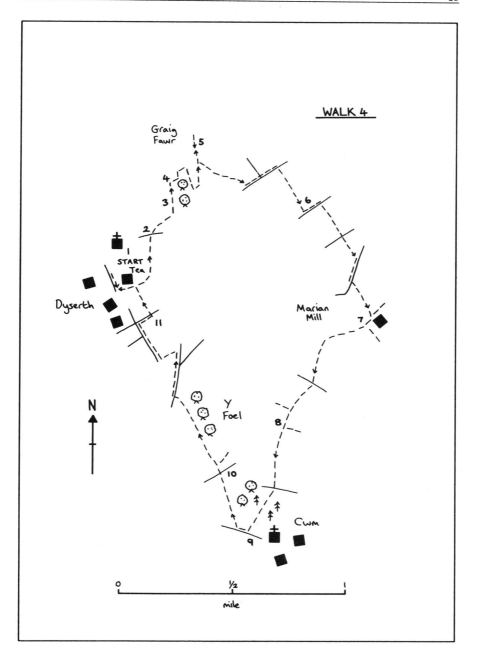

2. On reaching a lane, turn right and, in about 50 metres, when the lane bends right, turn left down steps to a road. Turn right and take the next road left. In approximately 30 metres bear right on a tarmac path between houses. Cross a stile and walk through the field. Go through a gap in a line of trees and bear left. In a few metres take a narrow path uphill through the trees. On joining a level path - another section of the leat - bear left.

    Across the fields on your left is the tall shell of the Clive Engine House. Built in the 1860s, it housed a massive steam engine which pumped water from the Talargoch lead and zinc mine. The high costs involved in removing the water which seeped into the shaft made the mine unprofitable and it closed in 1884.

3. Cross a stile and continue ahead beside a fence. At the end of the fence, ignore the gate ahead and turn right up steps to the Prestatyn Walkway.

    The Prestatyn Walkway lies on the former trackbed of the Dyserth Railway owned by the London and North Western Railway Company. It opened in 1867 to carry minerals from local mines and quarries. A passenger service followed, which operated from 1905 until 1930. A local landowner, H.D. Pochin, hoped the line would extend to Newmarket (now called by its old name Trelawnyd) and in 1884 he built the route as far as Marian Mills. LNWR was not persuaded and trains never ran beyond Dyserth. The disused railway line is now a recreational footpath and it forms a section of the North Wales Path, a long distance trail from Prestatyn to Bangor.

4. Turn left to cross a bridge above a lane and, in a few metres, bear right on a path and follow it uphill through trees. The lane is below on your right. Go through a kissing gate and, after passing a ladder stile and National Trust sign, turn left on a path uphill. Go through a kissing gate and take a path slightly to the right. Pass some rocky outcrops and, on reaching open ground beyond the trees, turn left through gorse bushes. Walk up the grassy slope to the trig point on the summit of Graig Fawr.

    Graig Fawr was bequeathed to the National Trust by Sir Geoffrey Summers of Shotton Steelworks. Old mineral workings lie below this great limestone hill, which is rich in lime loving plants. Wild thyme, lady's bedstraw and common rockrose may be found on the grassy slopes, and butterflies to be seen include the common blue. The summit of the hill is a fine viewpoint and views extend west across the Vale of Clwyd to distant Snowdonia. The nearest summit south is Y Foel. Beyond it is the forested Mynydd y Cwm. Meliden lies below Graig Fawr and on the coast sprawls Prestatyn. To the east is the wooded Gop Hill, which is topped by the largest tumulus in Wales.

Graig Fawr

5. Descend by the ascending route for about 100 metres. Keep ahead on a clear path to gates opposite a cream house with several brick chimneys. Go through a kissing gate and turn left on the lane. Pass some houses and ignore a lane on the left. In about another 40 metres turn right on the Offa's Dyke Path. Cross a stile above a drive entrance and keep ahead across the field to a stile. In the next field slant slightly left to a hidden corner. Keep ahead following a line of poles to a stile and lane.

6. Turn left and in approximately 150 metres cross a stile on the right. Walk uphill through the middle of the field to the next stile. Continue ahead, passing farm buildings on the right, to a stile near a gate. Cross the road to continue on the Offa's Dyke

Path. After crossing a stile, follow a field boundary on the right. When the hedge bends right, keep ahead to a stile. Turn right to follow the lane downhill and pass a cottage. Ignore a track on the right - a little way along it is a ruined corn mill, Grove Mill. Keep ahead on a rougher track. Pass Marian Mill Trout Hatchery on the left. On reaching a track junction at Marian Mill, turn right on a bridleway.

7.   Walk along the track and ignore a path on the left. In another 400 metres bear left over a stile. Keep ahead across fields to a lane. Turn left and, in approximately 20 metres, turn right over a stone stile onto the track for Tyddyn y Cyll. Follow the track and in about 120 metres, at an acorn symbol, bear left. Follow the hedge on the right to a ladder stile. Walk up the middle of the field to the next stile and a track.

8.   Leave the Offa's Dyke Path (which bears left) and cross the track to a footpath opposite. Walk directly across the field to a stile near a gate. Go up the field, slanting very slightly left to a stile. Follow the left boundary of the next field to a stile and descend steps to a lane. Cross the lane to another stile. Walk downhill to a stile in the right corner and descend a clear path through woodland. Cross a stile into a field and bear right a few paces before slanting left across the field to a stile near Cwm Church.

The English translation of Cwm is valley, an appropriate name for this pretty village. Dedicated to the Celtic saints Mael and Sulien, the church has a double bellcote. Look in the churchyard for the ornate hooded tomb of Grace Williams who died in 1642.

9.   Turn right along the lane. Before reaching a house on the right, bear right on a path going up to a stile. Walk up the field to a stile. Bear left along a path to another stile. From here there are fine views of the Vale of Clwyd. Walk uphill, veering very slightly right. Shortly you should be crossing the hillside slightly above a left-hand fence. Cross a stile next to a gate. Walk ahead, downhill now, and follow a right-hand fence. Views stretch north to the coast. Ahead is Y Foel. Cross a stile and emerge on a lane.

10. Turn left and, almost immediately, bear right up steps to a stile. Slant left to follow a clear path along the hillside of Y Foel. Enter a wood and continue on the path until it ends on an access lane.

Walk ahead to join a road and turn right. Ignore Upper Foel Road on the right and in about another 70 metres turn left on an enclosed path. Cross a road to follow another path and at the next road turn right. Pass a school and at a junction bear right to the ·crossroads.

11. Turn right and in about 30 metres, opposite the Cross Keys, turn left on a path that soon passes between walls. Join a tarmac path and bear left downhill. The path becomes rougher and descends through woodland. Descend some steps on the left and bear left at more steps to retrace the outward route to the waterfalls, café and car park.

5. Whitford

Route: This varied walk passes through the lovely meadows and woodlands of Downing, home of the 18th-century naturalist Thomas Pennant. There are splendid views and the route takes in a section of the Dee estuary.

Distance: 5 or 6 miles.

How to get there: North-west of Greenfield, leave the A548 for a road opposite Abakhan Fabrics. Ignore a lane on the left and, in another 600 metres, park at the end of the houses on the left.

Public Transport: Buses from Rhyl and Greenfield pass through Maes Pennant. Alternatively, start at Abakhan Fabrics, which is on the A548 and the Chester-Rhyl bus route.

Start: GR 166794. Hafod y Ddol, Maes Pennant. The starting point is at the west end of a narrow road which runs parallel to the main road through Maes Pennant.

Maps: OS Landranger 116 or OS Pathfinders 737 and 755.

The Tea Shop

Amongst the intriguing buildings of Abakhan Fabrics mill shop complex at Llanerch y Mor, you will find The Coffee Shop. Lead smelting took place on the site and the works had a huge waterwheel. There are fabric, wool and gift shops and a children's adventure playground. The Coffee Shop serves breakfast, lunches and afternoon teas. Jacket potatoes and home-made soups are on offer and there is a huge selection of baps and sandwiches as well as cakes. Open all year, seven days a week 9.00am until 5.00pm. On Thursdays it is open until 7.00pm. Tel: 01745 560312.

The Walk

1. From just beyond the houses on the south side of the road, follow a path to a small gate and bridleway. Walk ahead on a path between trees. This was once the approach to Downing. Go through a gate and continue through another field to emerge on

a lane. (If you turn left for a short distance, you will reach the entrance to Forest Hill Trout Farm which sells fresh trout and home-made jams. Cups of tea, coffee and home-made cakes are also on offer.)

2. Cross the lane to a stile on the right of a gate. Walk uphill on a broad track with a stream below on the right. Higher up you will pass the site of Downing Hall.

   Downing Hall was the birthplace of Thomas Pennant, the famous naturalist, historian and traveller. He is remembered today for his travels in Wales, but in the 18th century he was known in Europe for his work on zoology. His correspondents included the Swedish botanist Carl Linnaeus and Gilbert White of Selbourne. One of his ancestors was the last Abbot of Basingwerk Abbey. When sold in 1920, the Downing Estate consisted of over 12,000 acres, and the 17th-century hall had stabling for 12 horses. Two years later the mansion burnt down and it was demolished in 1953.

3. After passing a wall and buildings on the left, bear left. Cross a stream and follow the path to a stile and lane. On the right is Upper Downing, which is now a nursing home. Bear left and follow the lane to Whitford. Turn right to pass the parish church on your left.

   Dating from the 16th century, the Church of St Mary and St Beuno was largely rebuilt in the 1840's. Inside there is a 17th-century font, an old chest and a memorial to Thomas Pennant. In the churchyard is the grave of Moses Griffiths, the self-taught artist who accompanied Pennant on his tours and illustrated his books.

4. Continue along the lane and, shortly, turn right to have a school on the right and houses on the left. Cross a stile and bear half-left to a fence. Follow the fence on your left and ignore gates in it. As you descend there are fine views ahead of the Dee estuary, Hilbre Islands and the Wirral peninsula.

5. When you reach the corner of the field, go through a small gate and descend to cross a stream. Go up to another gate and emerge in a field. Bear diagonally left and follow a fence on the left. When it ends, continue across the field to a fence type stile. Keep ahead through Whitford Wood on a clear path. In approximately

600 metres it bears right to reach a fence corner. Follow the fence on your left to a stile. Walk across the field, with the woods on your left, to a stile and lane.

6. Turn right and in approximately 300 metres, opposite a field gate and walking man signpost, turn left on a clear footpath through the wood. Cross a small footbridge over a stream and continue with the stream on your right. A short stretch of the path can be slippery when wet. Ignore another footbridge and follow the path as it bears left and rises between a building and fence to a small gate. Walk ahead past a stone building to join a track and bear right to descend it. The track curves to the right and passes some houses. Ignore a road on the left and keep ahead. At the last house, go ahead on a path between hedges. Continue between fences to some woodland and descend steps to the car park at the Llety Hotel.

7. Cross the road with care and bear right to pass the Llety Hotel and a lane on the right. In another 100 metres, immediately after passing a house on the left, turn left on a narrow path. Cross a footbridge over the railway line. Continue beside a high fence on your left. At the end of the fence there is a stile and seat over-looking the Dee estuary.

In the winter the Dee estuary attracts thousands of waders, which come to feed on the shellfish and worms they find in the silts of the tidal waters. The estuary is also important for wildfowl. In the nearby fields, herons may be seen stalking the gutters.

8. Follow the track through a gate and continue beside the Dee. When you reach a track on your right, you have the option of shortening the walk by returning directly to the parking place, or having a longer walk beside the estuary to Abakhan.

9. **Shorter walk:** Turn inland to cross the bridge over the railway line. Turn left along the A548 and in about 100 metres, at the Glan y Don, bear right on an access lane. Pass some houses on the right and continue to Christ Church, which was built in 1844. Before reaching the church gates, bear right on a path that climbs alongside the churchyard. Shortly, turn right on another path. It climbs to pass between houses and emerges at your starting point.

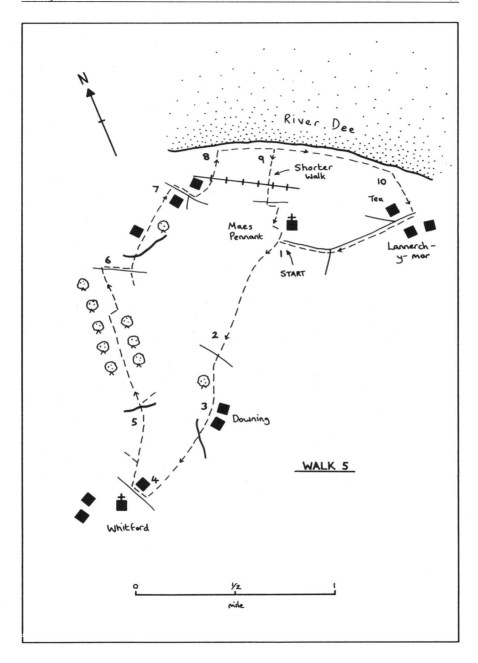

WALK 5

The moored Duke of Lancaster at Llanerch y Mor

Longer walk: Continue beside the estuary to reach gates at the moored ship, the Duke of Lancaster.

The Duke of Lancaster is a well known landmark on the coast between Greenfield and Mostyn. The vessel used to ply between Heysham and Belfast, but since 1979 it has been moored at Llannerch y Mor.

10. Bear right on a path to climb onto an embankment. Follow the path alongside the ship. At the end of a fence, descend to a track. Immediately, bear right and pass under a low railway bridge. Walk up to the A548. Turn right to Abakhan and The Coffee Shop. To return to your starting point, take the road opposite Abakhan, or retrace your steps along the estuary to the track seen earlier and follow the directions for the shorter walk.

6. Greenfield

Route: This is a fascinating walk, full of interest. Industrial archaeology, abbey ruins, a famous legendary well, a disused railway trackbed and a pretty wooded valley with several pools are features on this short walk. Allow plenty of time to explore.

Distance: 3 miles.

How to get there: Greenfield is on the A548, north Wales coast road.

Public Transport: Buses from Chester and Rhyl.

Start: GR 196774. Greenfield Country Park car park on the A548.

Maps: OS Landranger 116 or OS Pathfinder 755.

The Greenfield valley has attracted people since monks first farmed here and pilgrims visited the holy well. During the Industrial Revolution, the well's stream was used to power the waterwheels for the machinery of cotton and copper mills. Nowadays, the valley forms a picturesque, peaceful area of woodlands, reservoirs and industrial remains. There is also a visitor centre, and a farm museum with animals and old buildings.

The Tea Shop

Basingwerk Buttery is located close to the abbey ruins in the Greenfield Valley Heritage Park. Omelettes, Welsh rarebit and other hot snacks are on offer and, also, home-made scones, cakes and delicious teabreads. Open from Easter until 31 October 11.00am-5.00pm (4.00pm at the end of the season). Tel: 01352 714172.

The Walk

1. Follow a path that leaves from the back of the car park. Bear right to pass the ruins of Basingwerk Abbey.

    Benedictine monks founded Basingwerk Abbey about 1131 and a few years later it changed to the Cistercian order. The monks developed the

Ruins of Basingwerk Abbey

valley into a thriving agricultural community with corn and fulling mills, and they also worked mines in the hills near Holywell. Thomas Pennant, an ancestor of Pennant the naturalist, was abbot of the abbey at the end of the 15th century. After the dissolution of the monasteries in 1536, parts of the abbey were taken to other churches. The site was given to Henry ap Harry of Llanasa and, through marriage, it came into the hands of the Mostyn family of Talacre. They restored part of the abbey and lived there until the early 18th century, when it became disused. A large amount of the abbey stone was used to build the mills in the valley.

2.   Pass the Visitor Centre on your left, and turn left between buildings on a broad track. On reaching a lane, turn left. In a few metres you will pass a viewpoint of the Abbey wire mill weir. Continue to the Lower Cotton Mill.

Used mainly as a warehouse, the six storeys high Lower Cotton Mill was built in ten weeks in 1785. In the mid 19th century, the building became a flour mill.

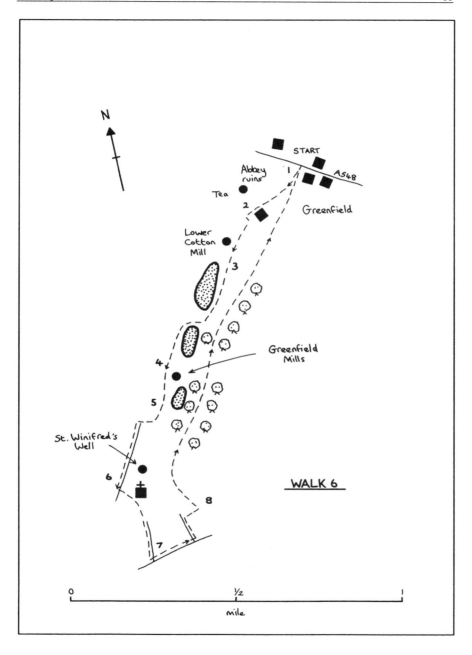

N

START
A548
Abbey ruins
Tea
Greenfield
Lower Cotton Mill
Greenfield Mills
St. Winifred's Well
WALK 6

0   ½   1
mile

3. When the lane goes uphill, continue beside a pool. Some ducks, grebes and swans may be present. Pass some picnic tables and, at a fork in the path, bear left up steps to a track. Turn right and pass the site of Meadow Mill, a mill which made copper rollers for printing on cloth. On reaching a junction of tracks, take the path that descends on the right. Cross a bridge and bear left on a path beside Meadow Pool.

4. Cross a car park and bear left through a kissing gate onto a broad track. Pass the clock tower and continue to a fork. Take the lesser path on the right and pass Greenfield Mills on the left.

    Greenfield Mills, the Battery Works, is the largest of all the industrial sites in the valley. Operating between 1766 and 1894, the works produced large amounts of brass and copper goods. Kettles, pans, bowls and other utensils were exported from Liverpool to the west coast of Africa, where the merchants traded the goods for slaves who were taken to the West Indies and America. After the closure of the works, some of the buildings were used for clothing manufacture until damaged by fire in the 1950s.

5. Walk ahead on the path and pass another pool on the left. Follow a stream and go through an arch. Turn right to pass the Royal Oak on the left. On reaching a road, turn left on the pavement to St Winifred's well.

    The holy well of St Winifred has not only made Holywell famous, it was also the main source of the valley's prosperity. The legend attached to the well began in the 7th century when the chieftain Caradoc tried to seduce the beautiful Winifred, a niece of St Beuno. When she rejected his advances and tried to escape, Caradoc chased after her and severed her head. Her uncle St Beuno replaced the head on her body and she returned to life. The only reminder of her decapitation was a white scar around her neck. Caradoc was swallowed by the earth and his relatives cursed. The holy well sprang up where St Winifred's head had fallen, and it became a great place of pilgrimage.

    The chapel surrounding the well is late 15th century and probably replaces an earlier structure. It may have been built for the mother of Henry VII, Margaret Beaufort. Basingwerk Abbey was granted the well and held it from 1240 until 1537. Many famous people visited the shrine, including Henry V, before his battle at Agincourt, and James II, who came in 1686 to pray for a son.

The constant flow from the spring attracted industrialists to the valley; it was reputed to produce copious amounts of water. In the early 20th century extensions of lead mines near the spring's source almost halted the flow, and the present day stream is much less than its former self.

6. Continue along the pavement and, after passing a chapel, turn left. Bear right along a path and continue ahead to pass flats on the right. Keep ahead to a road junction.

7. Turn left and, shortly, pass a car park. At its end, turn left down steps and walk downhill between two car parks. Pass Delyn Press Printers on the left and, in a few metres, turn right downhill on a steep tarmac path. On reaching another path, turn left under a bridge to pass the old site of Holywell Station.

LNWR opened a passenger line from Greenfield to Holywell Town Station in 1913. it was laid on the bed of an old mineral line and had a gradient of 1 in 27. The line closed in 1954.

8. The walk now follows the track bed of the old railway line. Ignore paths off and continue along the main track. On reaching the junction near Meadow Mill, continue ahead. Pass a field and farm on the right. Keep ahead at another junction and cross a footbridge. Descend steps to the path near Basingwerk Abbey. Turn left to The Buttery, or right to return to the car park.

7. Tremeirchion

Route: A lovely, varied and interesting walk with panoramic views. The route climbs gradually to follow a section of the Offa's Dyke Path and returns through a nature reserve.

Distance: 5½ miles.

How to get there: Tremeirchion is on the B5429 between Rhuallt (A55) and Bodfari (A541). In Tremeirchion take the Holywell road as far as the church.

Public Transport: One bus a day from Denbigh (No 40 to Rhyl). Buses every two hours (No 14) on the Denbigh-Mold route stop at Bodfari, 2 miles off route (from point 10).

Start: GR 083730. Tremeirchion Church. Roadside parking.

Maps: OS Landranger 116 or OS Pathfinder 755.

Tremelrchion is an attractive village on the western slopes of the Clwydian hills. The medieval church, dedicated to Corpus Christi, has several interesting items including stained glass and a canopied 14th-century tomb. In the porch a seat is formed from a 13th-century cross slab. An 800-year-old yew tree can be seen in the churchyard.

The Tea Shop

Fron Haul is a charming 19th-century farmhouse situated in lovely surroundings halfway through the walk. Mrs Edwards provides accommodation for those wishing to spend time in this beautiful area, and the farmhouse is a popular stop for walkers following the Offa's Dyke Path. Light lunches and afternoon teas are served to non-residents. The menu includes soup, sandwiches, cream teas and home-made cakes. Tel: 01745 710301.

The Walk

1. With your back to the church, turn left along the road. In about 100 metres, at a footpath signpost, turn left through a field gate. Walk directly ahead to a stile. Bear half right to cross another

stile and maintain this direction to the next stile. Ahead, visible above the trees on the skyline, is the little church belonging to St Beuno's College.

St Beuno's College was built in 1848 by J.A. Hansom, the architect who built Bodelwyddan Castle and designed the hansom cab. It was to be a training college for Jesuit priests and had a community of sixty people. A student at the college designed St Mary's Church, the church on the rock. Gerald Manley Hopkins, the poet, studied theology at the college from 1874 to 1877. Ill health meant he did not complete the four-year course, but he wrote some of

St Mary's church nestling in the trees

his finest poetry whilst staying at the college. St Beuno's is now a spiritual retreat centre.

2. Continue half right and walk downhill to a stile in a corner. Walk uphill with the field boundary on your right, passing a stile where the fence is broken. When a house is in view ahead, and the fence veers to the right, walk downhill to the right-hand corner of the field. Cross a stream and bear left to cross a stile. Pass in front of the house called Ysgubor and emerge on a lane.

3. Bear right along the lane and pass a house on the left. When the lane ends, continue on a grassy track. On meeting another track, bear right. Continue on the track when it joins the Offa's Dyke Path. When you reach a junction where two lanes meet, take the first (nearer) lane on the right.

4. On reaching a lane junction in 400 metres, bear left. In a few

metres, turn right on a lane. Stay on this lane for 500 metres and, at a point where it bends sharp left, keep ahead to cross a stile next to a gate. Follow the grassy path uphill, following the Offa's Dyke acorn waymarks. Bear slightly left to a stile. Cross the summit of Cefn Du by bearing slightly right to find a stile where three fences meet. From here there are fine views of the Clwydian range. Walk downhill on a clear path to reach a lane.

5. Turn right to follow the lane downhill. At crossroads turn left. On reaching another lane, turn right. In a few metres you will see the farmhouse refreshment stop, Fron Haul, on your right.

6. On leaving Fron Haul, bear right and, in about 250 metres, turn right on another lane. In 200 metres you will reach the crossroads met earlier. Turn left on a narrow lane, from which there are fine views of the Vale of Clwyd. After passing houses, the lane has a wood on the right. When the lane starts to descend more steeply at a left bend, take a narrow footpath on the right into the trees. Follow a fence on the left and cross a stile into a field. Bear left to emerge on a lane. Cross the lane directly to follow a track. When it bends right to a house, continue ahead on a narrow path. Cross a stile into Y Graig Nature Reserve.

The North Wales Naturalists Trust bought Y Graig in 1987. Scots pine and broad leafed trees cover the slopes of this limestone hill, whilst the craggy summit is open grassland. In spring, bluebells, wild garlic, wood anemone and dog's mercury may be seen in the woodland. Lime loving plants, including the common rock-rose, grow on the summit. On sunny summer days, butterflies such as the peacock, comma and small tortoiseshell flutter between the flowers. Woodpecker, nuthatch, tree creeper, goldfinch, goldcrest and other woodland birds may be seen on the reserve.

7. Bear right uphill beside a fence and in about 50 metres veer left towards crags. At a post with a white arrow, bear right to reach another post near a bench. From here there are extensive views over the Vale of Clwyd. Walk ahead towards some crags. Go up to the top of the crags and continue with a fence a short distance away on the right. When there are some trees ahead, bear left to a numbered post. A couple of paces before reaching it, veer left on a path that passes below the crags. In about 30 metres, turn right

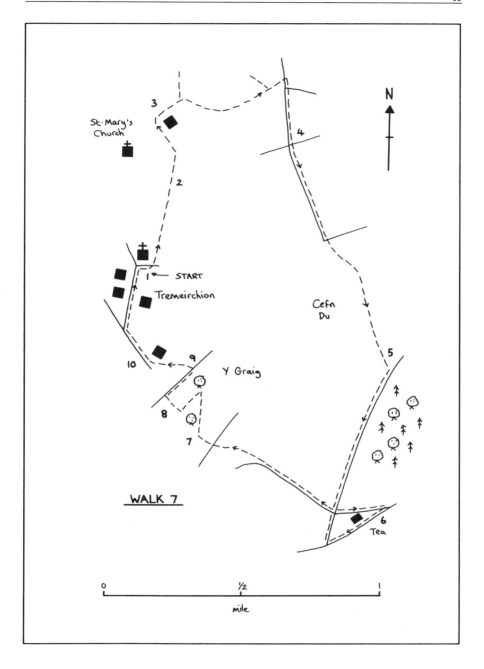

N

3

St·Mary's
Church
†

4

2

† START

Tremeirchion

Cefn
Du

10   9

Y Graig

8

5

7

WALK 7

6
Tea

0   ½   1
mile

on a path that descends into the woodland. The path swings right to a stile. Follow the path to a clearing and bear left between two tall beech trees. In another 100 metres, at a path junction, bear right and, shortly, leave the nature reserve through a kissing gate.

8. Follow a path to the left and emerge on a lane. Bear right, passing houses. At the end of the first field on the left, cross a stile. Across the fields on the right are the Cae Gwyn and Ffynnon Beuno caves.

    The Cae Gwyn and Ffynnon Beuno caves are situated close together in a limestone cliff. The large impressive entrance belongs to the Ffynnon Beuno cave. Excavations have revealed tools dating back 30,000 years and animal bones, including mammoth and hyaena.

9. Follow a fence on the right to a stile in the field corner. Bear left across the next field to a stile in the bottom corner. Follow the path through a garden to a stile.

    In an enclosure near the house, known as Ffynnon Beuno, is the holy well of St Beuno. Whilst a teenager, Henry Morton Stanley lived at this house with his aunt.

    Behind high walls on the opposite side of the road, is the large mansion called Brynbella, which was built for Hester Piozzi. She was a Salusbury, a locally important gentry family and her first husband was Henry Thrale, a brewer's son. Whilst living in London, she met Dr Johnson and their famous friendship lasted many years. After her husband's death in 1780, Hester Thrale married Gabriel Piozzi, an Italian musician. They moved to Wales and built Brynbella: the name is half Welsh and half Italian.

10. Turn right on the lane and, at a fork, go uphill on the road signposted Holywell. At the next fork, turn right to Tremeirchion Church and the start of the walk.

8. St Asaph

Route: This easy level walk follows lanes and field paths before returning along an embankment beside the River Elwy.

Distance: 3 miles.

How to get there: St Asaph is on the A525, and is bypassed by the A55.

Public Transport: Buses from Rhyl, Denbigh and Ruthin.

Start: GR 039742. Car park near the cathedral.

Maps: OS Landranger 116 or OS Pathfinder 755.

St Asaph originated in the 6th century when St Kentigern came to the area. A native of Scotland, he became Bishop of Glasgow and, after suffering persecution, he fled to the north of England and north Wales. He settled near the River Elwy and met a young monk called Asaph, whose family had also come from Scotland. They founded a monastery which Kentigern handed over to Asaph. The small settlement of Llanelwy grew around it and was not called St Asaph until the 12th century.

The present cathedral is the smallest in Wales and England. Its length is only 182 feet. Building started about 1240, but it was burnt by the soldiers of Edward I in 1282. After being rebuilt it was destroyed in 1402 by the Welsh troops of Owain Glyndwr. It was rebuilt in the late 15th century and has Victorian alterations by Gilbert Scott. On the Cathedral Green is the Translators Memorial, a monument to men who translated the Bible and Prayer Book into Welsh.

The Tea Shop

There are two possible refreshment stops:

The Farm Shop is a delicatessen that also serves hot and cold snacks. The menu includes soup. toasted sandwiches, baps, cakes and scones. Open Monday to Friday 9.00am-5.00pm. Saturday 9.00am-2.00pm. Tel: 01745 583553.

Turners Café is not a business enterprise, but a vocational training unit and part of the Pengwern College of Further Education (Mencap

National College). The varied menu includes home-made soup, stuffed jacket potatoes, sandwiches and a selection of cakes. Open Monday to Friday, 9.00am-4.00pm. Tel: 01745 583097.

The Walk

1. From the car park turn left to pass the cathedral. Go over the crossroads and continue along Mount Road. Stay on this road as it bears right to pass Fairholme School on the left. The road bends left and crosses a bridge over the A55.

   The lane offers fine views east of the northern end of the Clwydian hills. To the west is the marble church with its spire at Bodelwyddan.

2. Pass Pen y Bryn farm on the right and, when the lane starts to descend steeply, cross a stile on the right. Bear left alongside a hedge and cross a wooden fence into a small field. Continue beside the left boundary to the next field. Bear half right and go through a gap in the hedge.

3. Walk along the right-hand boundary of this field, beside a disused railway. when the field narrows, cross a wooden fence type stile and follow a hedge on your right towards a farm. Before reaching buildings, bear right through a gate. Immediately turn left to go through a gate into a yard. Go ahead between buildings to another gate and follow the farm drive to a junction with a lane.

4. Turn left a few paces then bear right up steps to cross a stile and footbridge over the River Elwy. Turn left for a few metres then bear right to ascend an embankment. Turn left to cross a stile and follow the embankment above the River Elwy. Cross an access drive and continue on the path above the river.

5. The path goes under the A55 and passes a livestock market. Shortly before a gate on the embankment, bear left on a path to walk closer to the river. Go up to the bank again and, before reaching the bridge over the river, bear right to a road. Turn left and follow it to the main road. Turn left to cross the bridge over the River Elwy. Follow the road uphill. You will pass the parish church on your left.

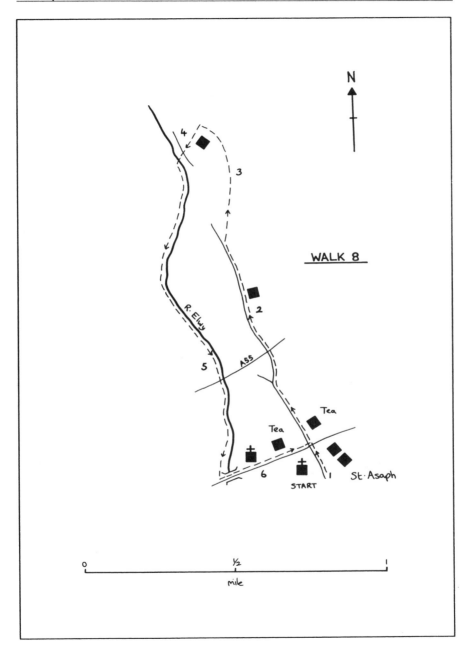

The parish church of St Kentigern and St Asaph is late medieval and has two naves of different periods. Both have hammerbeam roofs. The church contains the grave of the remarkable linguist Richard Jones. Better known as Dic Aberdaron, he was born on the Lleyn peninsula in the 1780s and spent most of his life wandering through Wales and England. He wore colourful clothing and carried a French horn around his neck. Although he could speak at least 15 languages, he remained poor. He lived for a few months in St Asaph before he died at the age of 63. The Welsh/Greek/Hebrew dictionary he compiled is in the cathedral. Opposite the church are the almshouses which were erected in the late 17th century for poor widows. They are now a restaurant.

6.   Continue uphill. The Farm Shop is on your left, whilst Turners Café is near the crossroads.

The footpath beside the River Elwy

9. Penycloddiau

Route: A long but gradual climb to the Offa's Dyke Path and Penycloddiau hill fort. There are superb views throughout the walk.

Distance: 8 miles.

How to get there: From Mold take the A541 in the direction of Bodfari to the lay-by 2 miles north-west of Nannerch.

Public Transport: Buses from Mold and Denbigh travel along the A541.

Start: GR 142711. Lay-by on the north side of the A541, ¾ mile south of Afonwen and 2 miles north-west of Nannerch.

Maps: OS Landranger 116 or OS Pathfinder 755 and 772.

The Tea Shop

Housed in a charming old mill, Edenshine Delights Restaurant forms part of the Afonwen Craft and Antique Centre. From 1786 to 1918 the building was a paper mill and produced high quality paper for £5 and £10 notes. Since then it has been a leather works and a woollen mill. Nowadays inside the building you can find a selection of craft and antique shops as well as the cosy restaurant. Everything at Edenshine Delights is homecooked and the varied menu ranges from three course meals to morning coffee and afternoon tea. There is a tempting selection of pastries, cakes and fresh scones with jam and cream. Open all year Tuesday to Sunday and Bank Holiday Mondays. Hours are 9.30am-6.00pm from Easter to the end of October. From November to Easter the restaurant closes at 5.30pm. Tel: 01352 720797.

The Walk

1. From the lay-by turn right (towards Bodfari) and in about 30 metres turn left on a lane. Walk uphill and pass Trefechan Farm on the right. Ignore a lane on the left and continue uphill for about 900 metres.

2. Turn left on another lane and ignore the track to Maes yr Esgob

on the left. On reaching Hendy and a cattle grid, bear right and continue past the next house, Hen Living. In about another 100 metres bear left on a track. Follow it below the hill called Bryn Golau and go through a gate across the track. Ignore a track on the left and at a junction fork left. Go over the crest of a hill and pass a cottage on the left. Ignore a track on the left and bear right to emerge on a lane.

3.   Bear right for about 100 metres to a point where two tracks meet the lane. Turn left through a field gate and bear slightly left to another gate. Follow the left-hand fence of the field for about 50 metres before bearing slightly right to a fence type stile next to a gate. Turn right on the lane and follow it uphill. At a junction turn right. In about a mile bear right into a forestry car park.

4.   Go through a small gate and follow a track to the right for a few metres before bearing right on a path with the acorn symbol of the Offa's Dyke Path. It rises steadily, following the edge of a forestry plantation. Cross a stile onto the open hillside and follow the waymarked path through grass, bilberry plants and heather to the summit of Penycloddiau.

Looking south along the Clwydian range from the summit of Penycloddiau

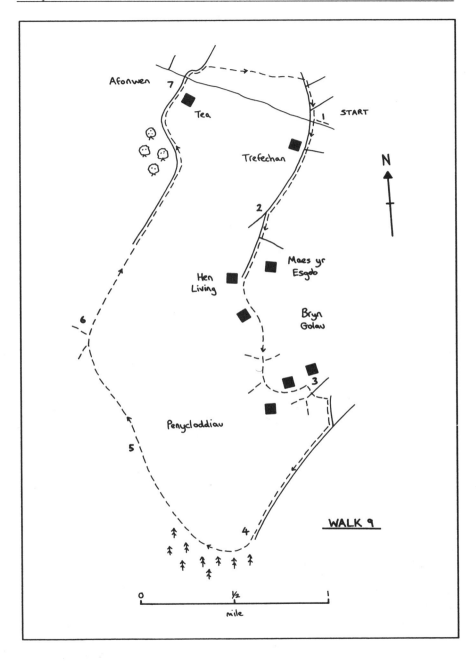

Afonwen 7

Tea

START

Trefechan

1

2

N

Maes yr
Esgob

Hen
Living

Bryn
Golau

6

3

Penycloddiau

5

WALK 9

4

0   ½   1
mile

Penycloddiau is the largest Iron Age hill fort on the Clwydian range. Triple earthworks surround an enclosure of over 50 acres. There are panoramic views on all sides. To the south are Moel Arthur and its hillfort, and the ruined tower on top of the higher Moel Famau. To the west are the fields of the Vale of Clwyd and, if visibility is good, Snowdonia's peaks in the distance. To the north the Clwydian hills continue to the coast and to the north-east the Wirral and Lancashire coast may be visible on a clear day. In spring and summer look and listen for wheatear, stonechat, whinchat and meadow pipit. Whilst descending the hill look for a memorial stone near a stile. It was erected in memory of Arthur Roberts MBE, a Ramblers Association member who was involved with the development of the Offa's Dyke Path.

5. Cross the ditches of the fort and follow the clear waymarked path downhill until you meet a track at some pines. Bear right over a stile and walk ahead. Ignore a track on the right. The walk now leaves the Offa's Dyke Path, which goes off to the left.

6. At first the track is fairly level, but it soon descends and joins a tarmac lane coming from a transmitting station on the left. Continue downhill and just before reaching the A541 you will see the entrance to the Afonwen Crafts Centre and the restaurant on your right.

7. Continue to the A541 and turn left. In a few metres take the first road on the right, which is signposted Babell. Pass some houses on the left and, where the road bends left uphill, cross a stile on the right. Follow the right boundary of the field and, when the fence bends right, keep ahead to a stile. Walk ahead to another stile. Continue on a clear path between bushes and small trees. Join a track coming from the right and keep ahead. Emerge on a lane and bear right. At a lane junction turn right to reach the A541. Turn left to the lay-by and start of the walk.

---

10. Denbigh

Route: Field paths descend to the wooded River Ystrad and a walk with literary associations. There are splendid views of the surrounding countryside. Some paths can be muddy after rain and there is a small amount of climbing.

Distance: 5¼ miles.

How to get there: Denbigh is on the A525 south of Rhyl and north of Ruthin.

Public Transport: Buses from Rhyl, Ruthin and Mold.

Start: GR 052661. Town car park signposted from Lenton Pool roundabout on the west side of the town.

Maps: OS Landranger 116 or OS Pathfinder 772.

Denbigh is the largest town in the Vale of Clwyd. The Welsh name Dinbych means little fortress. There is also a legendary explanation of the name. It was believed that a medieval knight called Sian Bodiau had magical powers because he had two thumbs on each hand. He killed a dragon who occupied the castle. When he returned with the dragon's head everybody shouted 'Dim Bach', meaning no dragon, and these words were later corrupted into Denbigh.

The Tea Shop

Situated in the High Street, The Forum serves main meals, afternoon teas and snacks. The varied menu includes salads, baked potatoes, toasties and sandwiches. There is a delicious selection of cakes, including chocolate fudge cake and bara brith. Open all year Monday to Saturday 9.30am-5.30pm. Sundays 12 noon-4.00pm. Tel: 01745 813449.

The Walk

1.   From the car park walk up to the High Street. Cross the road and turn left to pass the library on your left. Turn right uphill along Bull Lane. When the lane bends right, bear left at a corner to go

through a gap. Follow a railed path downhill and, shortly, bear right on a tarmac path. Pass a school on the left and the ruined Goblin Tower on the right.

2. Continue beside a fence and go through a kissing gate on the left. Pass through a similar gate and cross the field diagonally left to a corner where there is a kissing gate on the left and a stile on the right. Bear right to cross the stile and follow a hedge on your left to a tall kissing gate. Continue beside the left-hand fence and maintain your direction through a gate into the next field. Now walk beside a hedge on the right to a stile near a gate. Continue beside the right-hand hedge to another stile. Follow a path enclosed by bushes to a lane.

3. Turn right along the lane and in 150 metres bear left along a walled track. Pass a house on the right and continue on a narrow path through trees and bushes to a metal gate. Pass a fence and, when you join another path, look for a narrow path on the left that runs above the River Ystrad. With the river on your left, cross a stile into a field and walk towards a cottage. Cross a stile on the right.

4. Turn right along the lane and, shortly, bear left on a footpath. Pass a garden wall on the left and continue beside the river alongside woodland. Cross a stile near a gate and pass the ruins of Dr Johnson's Cottage on the right. Continue through a field to a stile at a field gate, beyond which there is a fork in the path. The walk follows the right-hand path, but to see Dr Johnson's monument take the left-hand path to a stile. The monument is at the bottom of the field near the river.

    Accompanied by his friend Mrs Thrale, Dr Johnson visited Gwaynynog in 1774 and, to mark the occasion, Myddleton erected the urn shaped monument. Dr Johnson considered it distasteful; an invitation to bury him alive. Dr Johnson produced several books including a dictionary of the English language.

5. From the path junction, go uphill on a path through the woods. Cross a stile into a field and bear right uphill beside the wood. On reaching the top of the field, bear right on a track that leads to a stile and gate. Veer left uphill on the track to the next stile. Cross the field to a stone stile and, shortly, cross another stile.

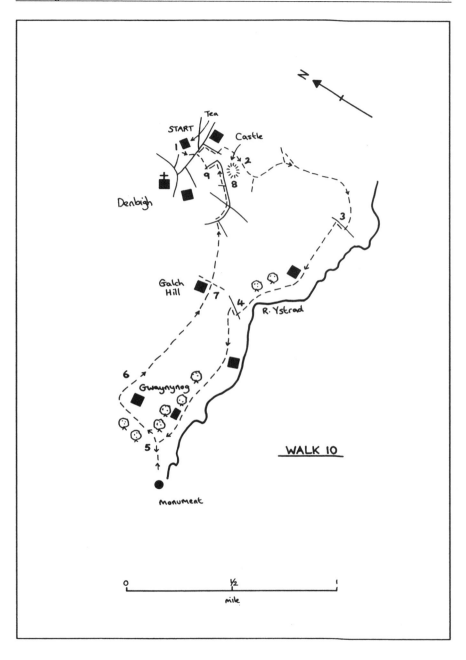

WALK 10

Follow the right boundary of the field to a stile near a gate. Walk ahead on the track and cross the access drive to Gwaynynog.

Originally the home of the Myddleton family, Gwaynynog was bought by an uncle of Beatrix Potter in the late 19th century. Beatrix visited the house and her illustrations in The Tale of the Flopsy Bunnies are based on the drawings she made of the walled gardens.

Looking back to the Ystrad valley from the footpath to Gwaynynog

6. Continue on the track through the middle of a field. When it enters another field, walk ahead on a grass track to a stile at a gate. From this point there are fine views of Denbigh Castle. Follow the left side of the field to the next stile and continue beside the field boundary to a stile at a black and white cottage called Galch Hill.

7. Pass Galch Hill on your left and follow the access drive to a stone stile on the left. Cross the field diagonally right to a stile in the top right corner. Follow the right side of the field to a stile and enclosed path that leads to a road. Turn left to a junction and turn right. At the next junction bear left and, shortly, take a lane signposted Castle.

The rock where Denbigh Castle now stands previously held the fortress of Dafydd ap Gruffudd, Llywelyn the Last's brother. He held it until Edward's final conquest in 1282. Henry de Lacy, Earl of Lincoln, was given lordship of the area and the building of new fortifications began that year. The town wall was probably built first and most of it still survives. The partly built castle was taken by the Welsh in 1294 and held by them for a short period. Owain Glyndwr raided the town in 1400 but failed to take the castle. There was more action in 1468 when the castle held out against the Lancastrians although the town was burnt. The walled town was not a success and by the mid 16th century it was becoming derelict. The inhabitants gradually moved downhill and established a larger town on the present site.

A cottage beyond the castle was the birthplace of John Rowlands who later changed his name to Henry Morton Stanley. As a small child, he was sent to St Asaph workhouse. Later, he ran away to sea as a cabin boy and took the name of a man who adopted him. He fought in the American Civil War and afterwards became a journalist. The New York Herald sent him to Africa to look for David Livingstone; no news had been heard of the explorer for several years. When he found him, he uttered the famous words: 'Dr Livingstone, I presume?' After Livingstone's death, Stanley went back to Africa and explored the Congo. On returning to Britain, he became an MP and a few years later he was knighted.

8. After viewing the castle, continue along the lane to pass St Hilary's Tower and Leicester's Church.

The tower is all that remains of St Hilary's Chapel, the church that was built in the 14th century for the inhabitants of the castle and walled town. The rest of the building was demolished in 1923.

After being granted the lordship of Denbigh, Robert Dudley, Earl of Leicester and a favourite of Queen Elizabeth I, intended to build a large Protestant church on this site to replace St Hilary's. Begun in 1579, it was abandoned five years later.

9. At the town walls bear left along Leicester Terrace and turn right onto a path into gardens. Descend to an alleyway that leads to the High Street in Denbigh. The Forum is on the opposite side of the road.

11. Loggerheads

Route: A lovely walk through woodlands is followed by an option to climb Moel Famau, the highest point on the Clwydian range. The shorter route involves little climbing and follows a bridleway through pleasant countryside before rejoining the longer walk. Only a very short section of the climb to Moel Famau is steep.

Distance: 6½ or 10 miles.

How to get there: Loggerheads is on the A494 between Mold and Ruthin.

Public Transport: Buses from Mold and Ruthin.

Start: GR 198626. Loggerheads Country Park car park, near the Visitor Centre.

Maps: OS Landranger 116 or OS Pathfinder 772.

The name Loggerheads is said to originate from a dispute concerning mineral rights and county boundaries. The area has been a beauty spot for over 200 years. Crosville bus company bought two fields and a wood at Loggerheads in 1926 and brought in more attractions. There were flower beds, a bandstand, swing boats, golf, croquet and a boating lake. Many people visited, using Crosville buses. Since being bought by the county council in 1974, it has become a country park.

Lead mining took place around Loggerheads for several hundred years prior to 1877, when the mines finally closed. In summer, the River Alun sometimes disappears through the swallow holes of its limestone beds and runs underground. This caused problems for the lead mines and a water channel was constructed to carry water along the valley. The 'leete' no longer carries water, but acts as a footpath. The park is rich in lime loving flowers and you may see enchanter's nightshade and dog's mercury. In the river look out for grey wagtail and dipper. Woodpecker, treecreeper, nuthatch, pied flycatcher and goldcrest may be spotted in the woodlands.

The Tea Shop

When Crosville bus company bought the land at Loggerheads in

1926, they built the first tea room here. In 1984, ten years after the land was bought by the county council, the original tea room was destroyed by fire. The new building provides a welcome refreshment stop for walkers in the country park. The varied menu includes hot meals, sandwiches and cakes. Open all year, seven days a week, 10.00am-6.00pm. Tel: 01352 810616.

The Walk

1. From the Visitor Centre turn left to pass the Outdoor Shop and cross a bridge over the River Alun. Turn left and follow the main path through the gorge. Go through a kissing gate and continue on a rougher path above the river. Pass some kennels and, at the end of the drive, cross a lane to a wide path.

2. Continue through trees and pass the entrance to some lead mines. Stay on the main path to follow the leete and cross the Devil's Gorge Bridge at another mine. The path is railed at one point where it passes above steep wooded slopes.

3. Emerge on a lane and turn left downhill. Cross a bridge over the River Alun and ignore a footpath on the left. Walk uphill and, where the lane turns right, bear left on the signposted path to Pentre. Follow the left boundary of fields until you meet a stile on the left. Continue beside a fence on the right to another stile. Walk downhill through woodland to a bridleway. Turn right uphill to emerge on a lane.

4. Turn left downhill and cross a river (Nant Gain). On reaching a junction, turn right on a lane unsuitable for wide vehicles. In 500 metres pass a grey Water Authority building on your right. Where the lane bends right, go ahead on a rough track for 350 metres to meet a track on the left. Here you have the option of a low level route or climbing Moel Famau.

5. **Low Level Route:**Turn left on the track and pass Cae Newydd and a track on the right. Follow the bridleway through a number of gates. Cross a marshy area and reach a stile at a gate. Continue on a wide enclosed path and, shortly, cross an open field. Pass a house on the right and go through a gate. In 150 metres, keep ahead at a bridleway sign. This is the point where you join the

route that ascended Moel Famau. Ignore all directions until point 8.

Moel Famau Route: Continue on the main track. Ignore a right fork to Garth. Walk ahead and when you reach a locked waterworks gate, bear left through a small gate. Follow a narrow path beside a fence. Keep ahead to cross a stream. At a bridleway sign go ahead on a path that slants to the right through bracken. On reaching a track, turn left and cross a stile onto the Offa's Dyke Path.

The Offa's Dyke Path runs through the Moel Famau Country Park. An impressive area of heather moorland, it is home to the red grouse. Other birds to look out for are buzzard, kestrel, wheatear, whinchat, and meadow pipit. To the west are splendid views of the Vale of Clwyd and distant Snowdonia.

6.   Turn left and follow the Offa's Dyke Path beside a boundary wall over Moel Dywyll. Stay on the main path and follow the acorn symbols for 1½ miles to the Jubilee Tower on Moel Famau.

At 1820 feet, Moel Famau is the highest point on the Clwydian range.

The Jubilee Tower on Moel Famau

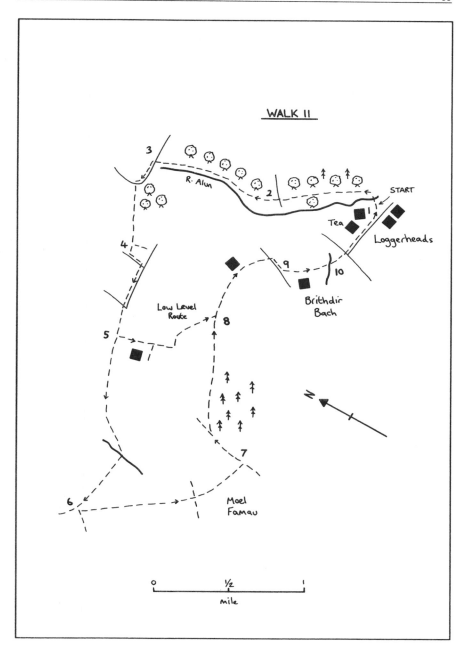

WALK 11

R. Alun

START

Tea

Loggerheads

Brithdir
Bach

Low Level
Route

Moel
Famau

0   ½   1
    mile

The summit is crowned with the remains of the Jubilee Tower. Designed by Thomas Harrison, it was erected in 1810 to commemorate the 50th year of George III's reign. It was built in an Egyptian style and had a base 60 feet square with a tower 115 feet high. About 5000 people walked to the summit on 25 October 1810 to attend the ceremony that laid the first foundation stone. In 1862 storms caused the tower to collapse. Renovation work has since taken place and there are information plaques on a viewing platform to help identify distant landmarks. On a clear day you can look west across the Vale of Clwyd to the peaks of Snowdonia; turning north you can see Liverpool and beyond; to the east is the Cheshire Plain.

7. Leave the tower in a northerly direction. Immediately veer slightly east to find a path that has a fence a short distance away on the right. Descend the path through heather to the edge of the forest. Continue downhill with the forest on your right. You will shortly have views of a reservoir below. On reaching a bridleway at a corner fence, turn right to have a low wall on the left and the forest on your right. Cross a stile at a gate and, shortly, reach a three way bridleway sign. Turn right to join the lower route.

8. Go through a gate and continue on a track enclosed by trees. Ignore a path on the left and join a track coming from Ffrith Farm. Continue on the track and pass a couple of houses. Emerge on a lane and turn right.

9. In approximately 200 metres bear left on the track for Brithdir Bach. Pass the farm and, at a fork in the track, bear slightly left to a gate. Follow the left-hand boundary fence through the fields. On reaching an open field, keep ahead. Shortly, follow the left-hand fence to enter a wood. Follow a path through the trees to a stile and cross some stepping stones over a stream.

10. Walk up to a wide track and turn left to emerge on a road. Turn right and in about 40 metres bear left on a lane. Walk downhill and, shortly before the end of the lane, take a path on the left to the car park and tea room at the Visitor Centre.

12. Ruthin

Route: A superb walk for a fine clear day. A steady climb through beautiful mixed woodlands leads to the Offa's Dyke Path and a splendid panoramic walk along the flanks of the Clwydian range.

Distance: 10 miles.

How to get there: Ruthin is on the A525 between Rhyl and Wrexham.

Public Transport: Buses from Rhyl, Corwen, Llangollen, Mold and Wrexham.

Start: GR 126585. Roundabout near the Craft Centre. Car parks nearby and off Market Street.

Maps: OS Landranger 116 or OS Pathfinder 788.

Standing on a hill overlooking the River Clwyd, Ruthin is an attractive old town and is named after its castle. The name means 'red fortress'. Edward I granted the lordship of Ruthin to Reginald de Grey. After the construction of the castle, the town developed to become an important centre for local industry. St Peter's Square was the market place. In the year 1400, Owain Glyndwr and his army marched to Ruthin on the eve of St Matthews Fair Day (21 September). The following day, disguised as peasants, they pillaged and burnt the town. The castle survived and during the Civil War was held for Charles I, but was taken by Parliamentary forces in 1646 and dismantled.

Beside Barclay's Bank in St Peter's Square there is a limestone boulder called Maen Huail. According to legend, Huail, brother of Gildas the historian, competed with King Arthur for the ladies and in a quarrel he wounded Arthur in the leg, giving him a permanent limp. Huail swore never to reveal what happened. Later, after Huail broke his oath and sneered at him, Arthur had his rival beheaded on this stone.

Located in the square and built in 1401 as a court and gaol, the National Westminster Bank has the remains of a gallows under its eaves. The last execution was in 1679. Founded in the early 14th century, St Peter's Church stands north of the square. It has a beautiful 16th-century carved oak roof, and the churchyard is fronted by

18th-century wrought iron gates made by the Davies brothers of Bersham. Behind the church is a close with buildings dating from the 14th century.

George Borrow (author of *Wild Wales*) walked to Ruthin from Llangollen and ate roast duck in the Wynnstay Arms in Well Street. At that time it was called the Cross Foxes.

The Tea Shop

The Bay Tree Restaurant is located in the Craft Centre, where you can see craftsmen at work and obtain tourist information. The varied menu includes home-made soup, salads, baked potatoes and a delicious selection of home-made cakes. Open all year Monday to Saturday 10.30am-5.00pm, Sundays 12 noon-5.00pm. Tel: 01824 705849.

The Walk

1. From the roundabout, walk up Market Street to St Peter's Square. Turn left to walk down Well Street and pass the

Ruthin's famous boulder below Barclays Bank

Wynnstay Arms on your right. Ignore a road on the left and keep ahead. Pass the Feathers Inn and follow the road as it bears to the right. Take a road on the left which is signposted Hospital.

2. In 600 metres ignore a left fork. Continue on the lane and pass Fferm Maes y Llan on the left. Emerge on the B5429 and turn right. In a few metres turn left on the track for Bathafarn Farm.

3. Pass the farm and follow the track to the waterworks buildings. When the track bends sharp left, walk ahead to pass a house on the right. This track becomes rougher and enters mixed woodland. In 800 metres ignore a track going to a house and walk ahead uphill. Go through a gate to have a field on the right. Moel Gyw is in view directly ahead and Moel Llanfair is to the right.

4. At Coed farm buildings the track bears left. Farther on, cross a stile to the left of a gate and enter a field. There are good views to the left of the Vale of Clwyd. Continue along the track. Go through a gate and immediately turn right to cross a stile and join the Offa's Dyke Path. Bear left uphill through the field and cross a stile in the middle of the upper fence. Continue ahead and cross two small hillocks. Descend to a stile near the left-hand corner of the field.

5. Walk ahead on a green track below Moel Gyw. There are superb views to the right of the Vale of Clwyd. Keep a look out for kestrel, buzzard and meadow pipit. In 900 metres the Offa's Dyke Path bears right on a narrow path.

    If you continue on the track for a few metres you will reach the Garreg Lwyd (Grey Stone) which marks an old route between Ruthin and Llanarmon. A path on the left - not a right of way but well used - leads to the top of Moel Gyw.

6. Follow the Offa's Dyke Path to a track and turn right downhill. Before reaching a gate, turn left over a stile. Walk ahead, with a fence on your right, on a path that contours the hillside of Moel Llanfair. Emerge on a rough track and turn left for a few metres. Cross the first stile on the right and follow a narrow path. With a fence on the left, walk uphill through bracken , heather and bilberry plants. Pass above a narrow valley and cross a stile. Ahead is a transmitter, and below on the left lies Llyn Gweryd.

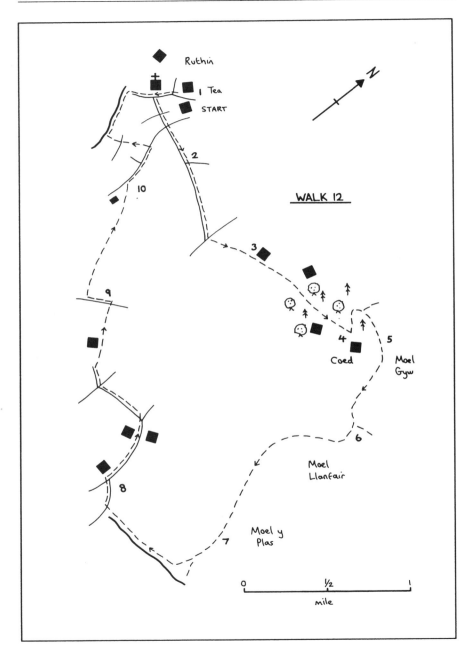

Ruthin

1 Tea

START

2

10

WALK 12

3

9

Coed

4

5

Moel Gyw

6

Moel Llanfair

8

Moel y Plas

7

0   ½   1
mile

7. Turn right for about 50 metres then bear left downhill to a ladder stile. Walk towards the mast, but, in a few metres, leave the Offa's Dyke Path by taking a path on the right. Descend towards a valley and cross a stile. Walk downhill on a clear path to emerge on a lane.

8. Turn right and in 400 metres ignore a lane on the left. Continue ahead and pass a farm on the left. Pass some pretty cottages and continue on the lane to a junction. Turn left in the direction of Llanfair Dyffryn Clwyd (Llanfair DC). Cross the B5429 and take the lane on the right signposted Llanfair DC. In 50 metres, where the lane bends left, keep ahead on a level track alongside trees. Pass the entrance to a farm on the left and follow the track between fields to a lane.

9. Turn left and in 250 metres, at a left bend, cross a stile on the right. Follow the right-hand fence through the field. Ignore a stile on your right. Maintain your direction through the fields until you meet two stiles close together. Ignore the right-hand one and cross the stile ahead. In a few metres cross a stile on the right and follow a left-hand hedge to another stile. Walk along the farm track to a road.

10. Turn right and follow the road for 800 metres. When the road bears to the right, turn left on a signposted footpath between fences. Cross a stile and follow the right-hand fence to a kissing gate and road. Turn left for about 100 metres and just beyond the drive to Scott House, cross a stile on the right. Walk beside the right-hand fence to a kissing gate on the right. It is near a weir and old bridge over the River Clwyd. Go through a short tunnel to a stile and follow a fence on your right to a park. Continue beside the river and walk through a car park. Turn right along Clwyd Street to St Peter's Square. Return along Market Street to the Craft Centre and restaurant.

13. Llandegla

Route: A lovely varied walk through limestone countryside and along the slopes of the southern Clwydian hills. The route follows a section of the Offa's Dyke Path and has splendid views.

Distance: 6½ miles.

How to get there: Llandegla is off the A525 and near the junction with the A5104 Chester road.

Public Transport: Buses from Wrexham and Ruthin.

Start: GR 196523. Llandegla car park opposite the memorial hall.

Maps: OS Landranger 116 or OS Pathfinder 788.

Llandegla is a small village situated in the attractive limestone countryside of the River Alun. In the 19th century it was an overnight stopping place for drovers taking cattle and other animals to markets in England. The village was also famous as the location of St Tegla's well which is said to be the oldest healing well in Wales and reputed to cure epilepsy. Sufferers carried out a complex ritual which included bathing in the holy well, throwing in pennies, and carrying a chicken around the well and churchyard. Women carried hens, men cockerels. The night was spent under the communion table with a Bible for a pillow. Through these rituals, epilepsy was transferred to the chicken and if it died the cure was considered successful.

Although rebuilt in 1866, St Tegla's Church has some interesting old features. Inside hangs an elaborate medieval brass chandelier, thought to have been in Valle Crucis Abbey near Llangollen. Near it is a Georgian painted window made for St Asaph Cathedral in 1800. A disciple of St Paul, St Tegla was a female hermit who became known for her healing powers. The church is usually open during the day.

The Tea Shop

There are two possible refreshment stops:

The **Gate House Cottage Café** can be visited during the walk. Built in 1650 as a toll gatehouse, it is located at the junction of the A525 and

B5431. A good-natured ghost has been seen in the building. Soup, salads, sandwiches and a selection of home-made cakes are on offer. Open Friday, Saturday, Sunday and Monday from Easter to October 10.00am until 6.00pm.

In the village, **Llandegla Post Office** has a small café and serves tea, coffee, cold drinks and snacks. Open 8.00am -8.00pm on Mondays, Tuesdays, Thursdays and Fridays. Hours on Wednesdays and Saturdays are 8.00am to 12 noon. Also open on Sundays 9.00am until noon. Tel: 01978 790234.

The countryside around Llandegla

The Walk

1. From the car park, walk towards the church and take a lane to the right of it. You are now on the Offa's Dyke Path. When the lane bends right, keep ahead. Follow a stony track downhill to a stile and continue ahead along the left side of a field. At the end of the field, ignore the footpath ahead and turn left to cross a footbridge over the River Alun.

2. Follow a fence on your right. At the top of the rise look for a stile

in the fence. Walk downhill with the fence now on your left. Cross a ladder stile and keep ahead to a stile and footbridge. Follow the left boundary of the field and, after crossing a stile, bear left. Pass through a gap into the next field and at its end, bear left to have a fence on the right. Continue on a clear path to the B5431.

3. The walk continues along the Offa's Dyke Path. Cross the lane to the track for Chweleiriog Lwyd. Follow the access track over two cattle grids. When the farm is in view, leave the track to follow the left boundary of a field. Walk uphill through the fields, crossing a number of stiles. In 400 metres the path bears left to follow a hedge. After crossing a couple of more stiles, pass farm buildings on the left and emerge on a lane.

4. Turn right and follow the lane uphill. It soon levels then starts to descend. Shortly, cross a stile on the left, near a gate, and leave the Offa's Dyke Path. Walk ahead to pass trees on the left, then slant to the right and descend towards the Vale of Clwyd. On reaching a path, follow it downhill to a stile. Continue downhill to a green track that runs alongside a fence.

5. Turn left to have a fence on the right and fine views of the Vale of Clwyd. On your left is a hill called Moel y Waun. In 900 metres, when the fence starts veering left to descend to a small quarry, bear left up the hillside. Keep above a fence bordering a line of gorse bushes. Go through a gap where there was once a gate and follow a track to the top of the ridge. From this point there are good views towards Llandegla and Llanarmon yr Ial. Leave the track to cross a stile and walk ahead downhill towards a house.

6. On reaching a fence behind the house, turn right. When the fence ends at a corner, keep ahead and follow the bank of an old field boundary. About 30 metres before reaching a wall, bear right uphill to a stile. Continue with a fence on the left. Descend the hill to follow another fence to a gate. Go through a strip of woodland to another gate. Keep ahead to join a track.

7. Bear right to follow the track behind Accre Hall. At a fork take the left-hand track. Cross a stile at a gate near a line of trees and keep ahead to go through (or climb over if locked) another gate. Continue on a clear track to a lane. Turn left and in about 800

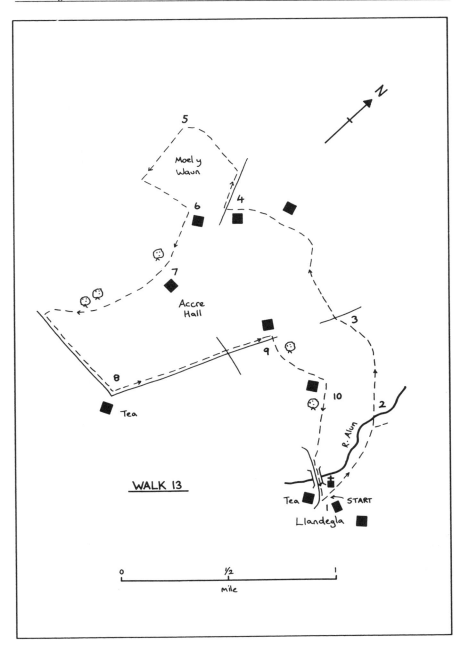

N

5

Moel y
Waun

6 4

7

Accre
Hall

3

9

8

Tea

10

2

R. Alun

WALK 13

Tea

START

Llandegla

0 ½ 1

mile

metres you can look across a field on the right to the site of Tomen y Rhodwydd, a motte and bailey castle.

Tomen y Rhodwydd is considered one of the finest medieval motte and bailey castles in Wales. Owain Gwynedd built it in 1149 during his conquest of northern Powys. The castle occupies a strategic position on the approach to the Nant y Garth pass through the Clwydian range. It was attacked and burnt by Iorwerth Goch ap Maredudd of Powys, but was later restored and occupied by the English in 1212, during the reign of King John.

8. On reaching the B5431, keep ahead a few more metres to the Gate House Cottage Café, which is on your right. After visiting the café, return to the B5431 and follow it in the direction of Llanarmon yr Ial. At a crossroads, continue ahead. In about another 500 metres, just before reaching a track to a farm on the left, turn right to cross a stone stile next to a gate.

9. Walk ahead on a track to follow a fence on the left. Stay beside when it bears to the left. In another 20 metres veer right to follow a line of trees and pass a hut nearby on your right. In 45 metres cross a track and bear slightly left to descend through trees to a stile in a fence. Go diagonally left to cross another stile. Bear left to pass a gate and follow a fence. Ahead and to the right, above the path, there is a ruined cottage. Pass below it, and, shortly, bear right uphill to a limestone ridge. Walk ahead and slant slightly left towards trees on another ridge. At a gap in the trees, ascend to a ladder stile.

10. Bear slightly left into another field. Walk downhill in the direction of Llandegla. Go through another gap and continue ahead through the middle of a long field. Aim towards the right of a house. Go through a stile next to a gate. Turn left along the lane. Cross a bridge over the River Alun and, shortly, reach the church in Llandegla. Turn right to the car park and post office.

14. Bryneglwys and Llantysilio Mountain

Route: Choose a clear day for this lovely walk. The views are spectacular. Paths and tracks ascend to a hill pass and a panoramic walk on a permissive path along the ridge of the heather covered Llantysilio Mountain. Some sections of the walk are steep.

Distance: 5½ miles.

How to get there: Bryneglwys is on the A5104 between Chester and Corwen. Approaching from Chester, Tyn Rhos is on the right about 600 metres before the turn-off to Bryneglwys village.

Public Transport: Infrequent buses from Wrexham and Corwen.

Start: GR 154480. Tyn Rhos. Walkers who will be visiting the tea room may leave their cars in the small car park or on the shingle near the farm track if the car park is full.

Maps: OS Landranger 116 or OS Pathfinder 805.

Bryneglwys is known for its connection with Yale, the American university. About two miles north-east of the village stands Plas-yn-Ial, ancestral home of the Yale family. Thomas Yale emigrated in 1637 and his son Elihu was born in Boston, Massachusetts. Elihu returned to Britain and after joining the East India Company, he later became governor of Fort Madras. He made a fortune and, on receiving an appeal for help in the foundation of a college in America, he sent a cargo of books and some Indian goods which were sold for about £562. In appreciation of his help, the college was named after him. The 15th-century church in Bryneglwys is dedicated to St Tysilio, a 6th-century saint. Inside the Yale chapel there is a memorial slab brought from Valle Crucis Abbey.

The Tea Shop

Tyn Rhos Farm is located near the A5104 north of the range of hills known as Llantysilio Mountain. The tea room is in the bungalow to the left of the farm track. Light lunches, snacks and cream teas are available. There is an excellent selection of homebaked cakes. Open every weekend from May to October 9.30am until 5.00pm. In high summer the tea room is usually open seven days a week and may not close until 7.00pm. Opening hours are flexible and if you wish to visit out of season, or on weekdays, arrangements may be possible if you phone in advance of your arrival. Tel: 01490 450286.

The Walk

1. From Tyn Rhos, walk out to the road and turn right along the grass verge. In about 400 metres turn left on a lane. Ignore a lane on the right and walk uphill to a junction.

2. Cross the lane and go through the gate directly opposite onto a track signposted Moel y Gamelin. Walk up the track and cross a stile at a gate. Ignore the stile on the right. Turn left and in a few metres bear right uphill. As you walk up the hill, bear slightly left to a stile in the top fence. Cross the next field by slanting left to a stile and emerge on a grassy track.

3. Bear right and go through a gate. Watch for buzzard, raven and peregrine overhead. The track ascends gently through the heather to a pass and track junction below Moel y Gamelin. This is an ancient route between Bryneglwys and Rhewl in the Dee valley. The walk bears right at this point , but you have the option of climbing the steep path on the left to the cairn on Moel y Gamelin. The views are worth the climb.

    At 1896 feet, Moel y Gamelin is the highest top on the range of hills known as Llantysilio Mountain which stretch from the Horseshoe Pass to Carrog, near Corwen. The summit is crowned by a tumulus erected about 2000 BC and a more modern cairn. From this point there are spectacular views east to the limestone escarpment on Eglwyseg Mountain, south to the Dee valley and north to the Clwydian hills. To the west are the Berwyn Mountains, the Arenigs and Snowdonia. Motorcyclists are responsible for the erosion on Llantysilio Mountain.

4. Return to the pass and follow the ridge by climbing to the hill fort on Moel y Gaer.

    The Iron Age hill fort on Moel y Gaer is thought to date from about 600 BC. A single bank surrounds the fort and it has a ditch on the north side.

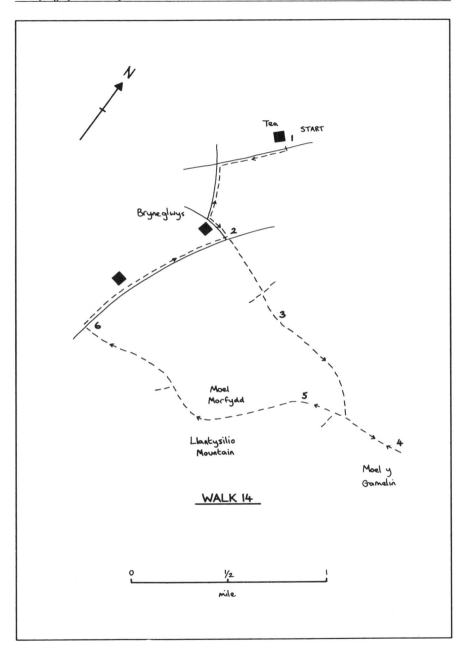

WALK 14

It is impossible to detect any hut platforms because of the dense cover of heather and bilberries.

Llantysilio Mountain

5. The path descends and then rises again to Moel Morfydd (1801 feet). Continue along the ridge by descending the hill. In about 300 metres, where the gradient eases, take a path on the right. It descends gradually to a lane.

6. Turn right and in about 450 metres the lane crosses a cattle grid. Continue on the enclosed lane and pass Ty Newydd Farm on the left. On reaching the signposted track you followed earlier, turn left and retrace your steps to Tyn Rhos.

15. The Horseshoe Pass

Route: A splendid walk for a fine clear day. The route includes some lane walking, and a steady climb through fields and moorland. Throughout the walk there are spectacular views.

Distance: 5 miles.

How to get there: The Horseshoe Pass is on the A542 between Llangollen and Ruthin.

Public Transport: Infrequent buses from Llangollen to Pentredwr (Point 3 on the walk).

Start: GR 192481. Car park at the top of the Horseshoe Pass, opposite the Ponderosa Café.

Maps: OS Landrangers 116 and 117 or OS Pathfinders 805 and 806.

On the climb to a break in the hills north-west of Llangollen, the Horseshoe Pass road curves around a wide valley to form the shape of its name. Almost any spot in this spectacular landscape offers dramatic views. Heather, bilberry and cowberry cover extensive tracts of moorland, providing a habitat for red grouse. In the 19th century several hundred men were employed in the slate quarries on Maesyrychen Mountain. The pass is often blocked by snow in winter.

The Tea Shop

Situated on moorland at the top of the Horseshoe Pass, the Ponderosa Café is a popular refreshment stop for tourists and walkers. There is seating outside. The varied menu includes hot meals, sandwiches and a selection of cakes. Usually open all year, but check in the winter. Hours on weekdays are 10.00am until 6.00pm. At the weekend the café opens at 8.00am and may stay open later than 6.00pm. Tel: 01978 790307.

The Walk

1.   From the car park at the top of the Horseshoe Pass, cross the road

and join a minor road behind the Ponderosa Café. Bear right and follow the old road downhill. Cross a cattle grid and in approximately 150 metres turn right on a track.

2. Follow the track to a fork. Turn left and in about 80 metres cross a stile on the left. Walk downhill towards the village of Pentredwr. Go through a gap in the trees ahead and slant right towards a corner fence. Look for a ladder stile below some trees. Follow a fence on the left and, shortly, emerge on a drive near a house. Follow the drive to a lane.

3. Bear right and in a few metres turn left through the village of Pentredwr. Ignore a lane on the left and at the next junction turn left in the direction of World's End. The lane bears right and as you proceed there are fine views south to Valle Crucis and east to Eglwyseg Mountain. In just under a mile the lane passes above a farmhouse on the right. In a few metres turn left on a track that enters a wood.

4. Follow the track as it rises above the lane. On reaching a track junction, continue ahead uphill. In approximately 150 metres,

This walk gives fine views of the Eglwyseg cliffs

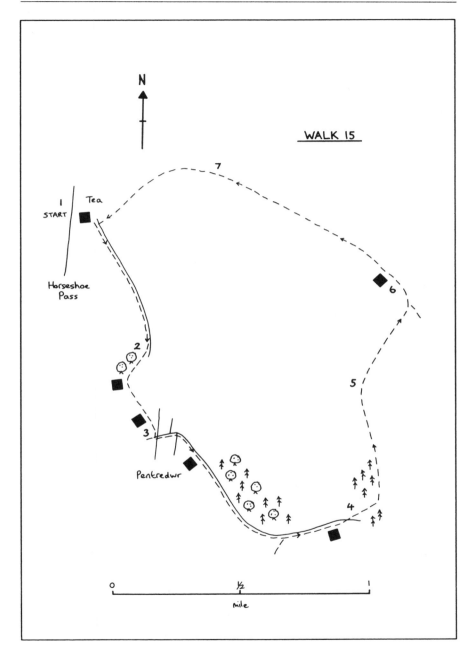

bear left with the main track. A field is now slightly below on the right. Go through a gate and follow the enclosed track uphill beside the forest. To the right are good views of the Eglwyseg escarpment and, in the foreground, the wooded hill called Gribin.

5. The track passes the disused Abergwern quarry and enters a field. Cross the field by bearing slightly right to the top right-hand corner. Go through a gate and follow a fence on the right for about 20 metres to a stile. Cross and slant left to another stile in the top right-hand corner. From here there are fine views towards World's End.

6. Turn left on a wide green track. In a few metres at sheep pens keep to the left. Cross two stiles and follow a left-hand fence for about 100 metres to a corner. Bear left to pass a ruin. In another 50 metres, leave the fence and maintain your direction uphill through open land. Look and listen for skylark, meadow pipit, wheatear and curlew. Head in the direction of a rock that points to the left. Pass above it and follow the clear path through low lying gorse. Stop frequently to enjoy backward views. Ahead, the transmitter on Cyrn y Brain is high above to the right.

7. At a fork, where a path goes ahead, bear to the left. In about 150 metres you will pass steep slopes above a valley. The path reaches a fence and follows it for about 100 metres before leaving it to emerge on a track. Turn left for approximately 300 metres. When the track veers away from the left-hand fence, continue on a clear path. Follow the fence on your left until you reach a stile near the old road. Cross the road to the Ponderosa Café and car park.

16. World's End

Route: An exhilarating walk following a section of the Offa's Dyke Path across the screes below Eglwyseg Mountain. The route uses good paths but it should be avoided in wet or windy weather. The second half of the walk offers superb views from the opposite hillside.

Distance: 6 miles.

How to get there: Take minor roads to World's End from Llangollen or Minera.

Public Transport: Nearest buses are to Llangollen, 3 miles from Point 4.

Start: GR 232483. Small car park in the forest up the lane from World's End.

Maps: OS Landranger 117 or OS Pathfinder 806.

The Tea Shop

Situated in the lovely Eglwyseg Glen, Eglwyseg Tea Rooms provides a welcome break halfway through the walk. Jacket potatoes, salads, sandwiches, home-made cakes and cream teas are offered. Open from the beginning of April to the middle of October on Fridays, Saturdays, Sundays and Bank Holiday Mondays. Hours 11.00am until 5.00pm. Bed and breakfast is also available. Tel: 01978 861591.

The Walk

1. From the car park, walk out to the lane. Turn right and follow it downhill. Cross a ford and ignore the stile that is on your immediate left. Bear right with the lane and turn left over the next stile onto the Offa's Dyke Path. Follow a clear path through coniferous trees and emerge on the open hillside below the Eglwyseg crags.

    The limestone cliffs and crags of Eglwyseg Mountain wind for three miles above long, steep scree slopes, forming a spectacular contrast to the green fields and woodlands below. Keep a look out for raven, buzzard and peregrine.

2. Continue on a clear path to another stile. It then follows a fence and, shortly, bears left uphill. The path becomes fairly level and there are superb views of the Eglwyseg cliffs above and ahead. Cross some long stretches of scree. At intervals along the route there are posts bearing the acorn symbols of the Offa's Dyke Path.

3. About 1½ miles from leaving the road, the path descends to a fence. After crossing a stream, be careful that you take the path that rises away from the fence. Cross an-other slope and de-

Offa's Dyke Path below the Eglwyseg cliffs

scend gradually in the direction of a house. On reaching a fence, keep ahead and, shortly, continue along the access track coming from the house.

4. Emerge on a lane and turn right. Ignore a lane on the left. Cross a bridge and bear right. Ignore a lane on the left. On your right you will see the entrance to the Eglwyseg Tea Rooms.

5. From the Tea Rooms, continue along the lane with woods on your left. In about 200 metres cross a stile on the left. The path rises through the wood and enters a field. Continue on a clear path with fine views on your right of the escarpment. Keep ahead to a gate and stile. Bear right to have a wood nearby on your right.

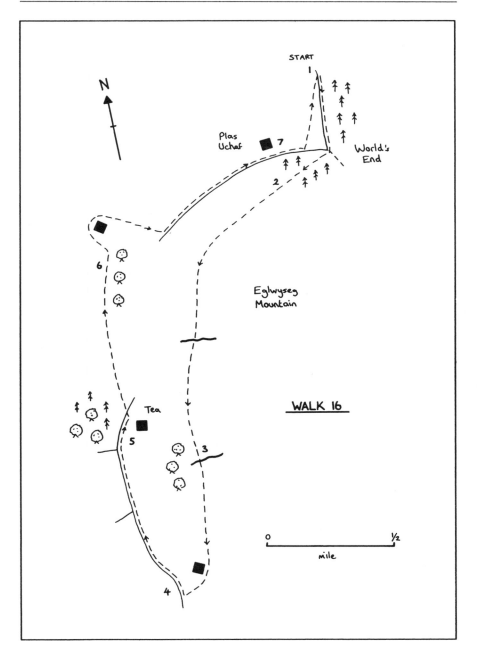

6.   Cross a stile between two gates and emerge at a bend on a stony track. Take the right-hand lower fork and follow it downhill. Pass a house on the right and continue on the track as it bears right. Follow it to a lane and turn left. In about 800 metres you will see Plas Uchaf manor house on the left.

Plas Uchaf is an Elizabethan half-timbered manor house. It is on the site of a former hunting lodge owned by Cadwgan, Prince of Powys. In 1108 his son Owain kidnapped Nest, the wife of the Norman lord Gerald of Pembroke and hid her in this remote valley. Owain was forced to flee, and although Nest was returned, Owain was killed a few years later.

The present house is mainly 16th century. In the Civil War Colonel John Jones, brother-in-law of Oliver Cromwell, lived here. Being a signatory to the death warrant of Charles I, he was executed on the Restoration of the monarchy.

George Borrow (author of Wild Wales) came this way in the 19th century on a walk from Llangollen to Wrexham. He called at Plas Uchaf to check the way and asked the name of the enormous rock ahead. He was told it was Craig y Forwyn, Maiden's Crag. The name may refer to its shape or the legend of a young girl in love who jumped from it to her death. When George Borrow reached the moorland, he took the wrong path and had to struggle through knee deep heather and quagmires before arriving in Wrexham.

7.   Continue on the lane. A few metres before reaching the ford, and where a stream crosses the lane, turn left to cross a stile that has a white waymark. Follow the path beside the stream and soon bear left on a path uphill. Follow a fence to a kissing gate on the left. Continue with the fence on the left. Go up steps to a stile and keep ahead on the path until it bears right to a stile. Turn left on the lane to return to the car park and starting point.

17. Panorama Walk

Route: This lovely walk follows permissive paths to limestone escarpments and moorland above the Vale of Llangollen. There is one long gradual climb and a shorter steep one. Views throughout the walk are spectacular.

Distance: 4 miles.

How to get there: Leave the A539 in Trevor at the Australia Arms. Ignore a lane on the left and bear right through Garth. Take the next lane left to a junction. Turn left to cross a cattle grid. In about 100 metres there is a parking area on your right.

Public Transport: Buses from Wrexham, Llangollen and Barmouth stop in Trevor, 1½ miles from the start.

Start: GR 247428. Car parking area below the monument on the Panorama Walk road. This is opposite the stile where the Offa's Dyke Path emerges from the wood.

Maps: OS Landranger 117 or OS Pathfinder 806.

The Tea Shop

Located above the Vale of Llangollen, Prospect Place Tea Room is in a lovely position, just off the Panorama Walk road. Refreshments can be taken in the tea room or at tables in the garden. Salads, baps, sandwiches, savoury scones and a delicious selection of home-made cakes are on offer. Open from Easter until the end of October Wednesdays, Thursdays and Fridays 12 noon 5.00pm. Saturdays, Sundays and Bank Holidays 10.30am-6.00pm. Closed on Mondays and Tuesdays. Tel: 01978 821602.

The Walk

1. From the parking area turn right and walk along the road with the woods on your left and the hillside on your right.

   This road is called the Panorama Walk and, beyond the end of the trees, views open up across the Vale of Llangollen.

View from the terrace above Trevor Rocks

Ignore a path on the right near an Offa's Dyke signpost. Continue along the lane for about 800 metres to a point where it bends to the left as it crosses a stream.

2.   Leave the lane to bear right on a wide path signposted 'Panorama'. Follow it uphill to a gate. Do not go through it but veer to the left and continue uphill beside a fence on the right. In about 600 metres you will reach a grassy terrace above Trevor Rocks.

From the limestone terrace there are superb views of the castle ruins on Dinas Bran, the Vale of Llangollen, Llantysilio Mountain and the Berwyn. Keep a look out on the walk for ring ouzel, wheatear, buzzard and small mammals including stoats.

3.   Continue along the terrace and, when the fence ends, keep ahead to a footpath signpost at a junction of paths above a valley. Turn right uphill and cross a stile.

4.   Turn right and follow a path above the remnants of the Eglwyseg Plantation. At the end of the trees, cross a ladder stile on the right and turn left. Descend a clear grassy path through patches

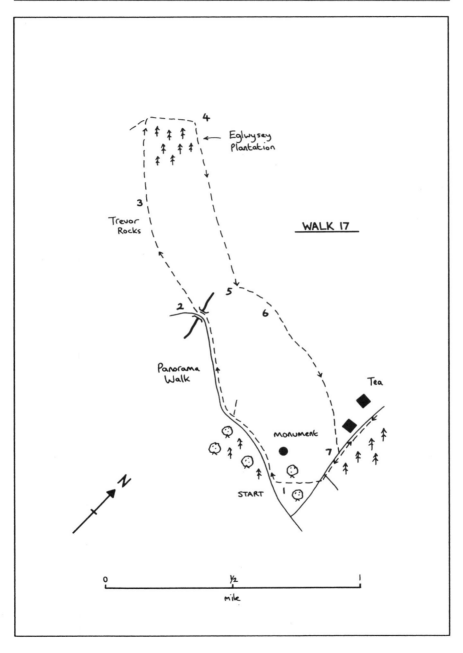

of gorse. To your right are fine views of the Vale of Llangollen. Cross a stile and continue on the path until a fence on your left ends at a corner near a footpath signpost.

5. Turn left uphill beside the fence. (If you continued along the lower path it would return you to the lane.) At the top of the hill, bear right to have a fence on your left. Follow a path through a broken wall to a footpath signpost. The walk turns left here, but you may like to walk ahead a short distance beside the wall to a point where you have fine views of the Pontcysyllte Aqueduct.

6. At the signpost, turn left downhill beside the fence to a gate near a corner. Bear right on a path, which follows a fence at variable distances. Shortly before reaching a farm, the path swings right. Cross a stile and emerge on a lane.

7. To visit the tea room, bear left on the lane for approximately 300 metres to reach the drive to Prospect Place Tea Room, which is on your left. To return to the parking area, turn right at the stile and follow the lane for 200 metres to a footpath signpost and stile on the right. Follow the main path through heather, bilberry plants and silver birch trees. Ignore a permissive path on the right. Descend to the parking area at the path to the monument.

The monument on the hillside is to I.D. Hooson, a bard who lived 1880-1948. From this spot the atmospheric views of Dinas Bran are especially magnificent at sunset.

18. Llangollen

Route: This lovely walk has many interesting features. An easy stroll along the Llangollen Canal is followed by riverside, woodland, and hillside paths with a final short, steep climb to the ruins of Castell Dinas Bran. Views of the surrounding countryside are superb.

Distance: 7 miles.

How to get there: Llangollen is on the A5.

Public Transport: Buses from Wrexham, Chirk and Barmouth.

Start: GR 214420. Car park in Market Street.

Maps: OS Landrangers 117 and 125 or OS Pathfinders 805 and 806.

Llangollen is a charming small town situated on the banks of the River Dee. It is famous for the International Music Eisteddfod which takes place every July when more than 12,000 amateur competitors perform in the pavilion. The town's name comes from St Collen who, according to legend, was one of King Arthur's knights. He eventually settled in the Vale of Llangollen and built a church near his cave. The present church dates from the 13th century and has a splendid hammerbeam roof.

The famous Ladies of Llangollen are buried in the churchyard. They eloped from Ireland in the 18th century and lived together at Plas Newydd with their maid. Many people sought their acquaintance and their visitors included Wordsworth, Lord Byron, Sir Walter Scott and the Duke of Wellington. The house and grounds are open to the public.

George Borrow spent a lot of time in Llangollen, and an account of his stay, including his ascent of Dinas Bran, can be read in his book 'Wild Wales'.

The Tea Shop

From the many tea rooms in Llangollen, I have chosen the Cottage Tea Rooms in Castle Street Square. The building dates from the early 19th century when it was two cottages. Lunches, Cottage Tea, and Welsh Farmhouse Tea are on offer and there is an excellent selection of cakes, including bara brith. Open February to Christmas 10.00am-5.00pm, sometimes later in the summer. Open weekends only from October until Christmas. Tel: 01978 860976.

The Walk

1. From the car park turn right to reach a crossroads. Turn left through the main street and cross the bridge over the River Dee. Originally a 14th-century packhorse bridge, it was one of the Seven Wonders of Wales. At the road junction, cross the road and bear left for a few metres. Shortly bear right on a path uphill to the Llangollen Canal. Turn left on the towpath and follow it under some bridges. Continue beside the canal to pass the Llangollen Motor Museum and the Chain Bridge Hotel. Follow the canal to the sluice gate and bear right to the Horseshoe Falls.

    Thomas Telford constructed the Horseshoe Falls in the early 19th century to feed water from the River Dee into the Llangollen Canal. The falls also provide some of Cheshire's water supply.

2. Walk through the field beside the River Dee and pass through a kissing gate. Follow a path to Llantysilio Church.

    St Tysilio's Church dates mainly from the 15th century. It has a medieval roof and an oak eagle lectern. The north window has some 15th century glass, including a figure of St James of Compostella. From May to September the church is open on Wednesday, Saturday and Sunday afternoons.

3. Walk out to the lane and turn right. Pass a car park on the right and ignore a footpath on the left. After passing a road junction on the right, turn left on a narrow lane. Immediately bear right on a path signposted Velvet Hill and Valle Crucis Abbey. Go up to a stile and bear right on a clear path along the side of Velvet Hill. Stay on the main path, which descends and continues beside a fence. At a footpath signpost go downhill and bear right to a stile.

4. Turn left along the road and in about 40 metres go through a kissing gate on the right. Cross the field to another kissing gate and turn left on an access lane to pass the entrance to Valle Crucis Abbey.

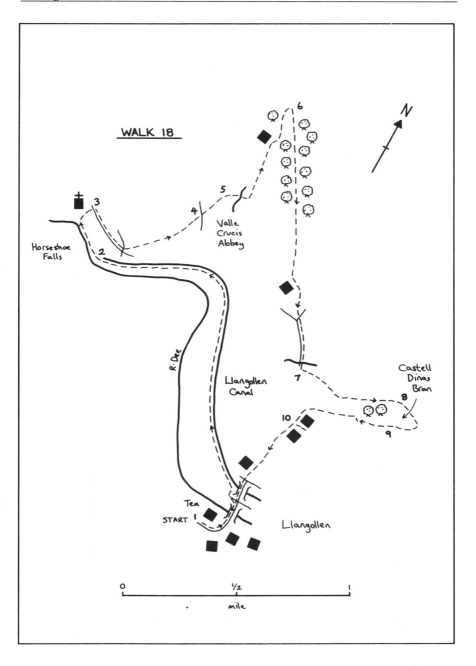

WALK 18

Horseshoe
Falls

R. Dee

Llangollen
Canal

Valle
Crucis
Abbey

Castell
Dinas
Bran

Tea
START

Llangollen

N

0   ½   1

mile

Valle Crucis means valley of the cross; the cross being the nearby Eliseg's Pillar. The Cistercian Abbey was founded in 1201 by Madog ap Gruffudd, the Prince of northern Powys. One of the finest parts of the abbey is the 15th-century vaulted chapter house, which has tracery windows. Above it is the monks' dormitory. Behind the east front of the abbey church is the monastic fishpond, the only surviving one in Wales. Valle Crucis is open from May-September 10.00am-5.00pm and there is an admission charge.

Approximately 200 metres north of the abbey, off the A542, the remains of Eliseg's Pillar stands on a low burial mound. When first erected it would have been much taller, possibly more than twice its present height. The much weathered inscription celebrates the names and glories of the ruling house of Powys. It was probably erected in the 9th century by Cyngen in memory of his great grandfather Eliseg. Cyngen died whilst on a pilgrimage to Rome. The cross was pulled down in the Civil War and before this piece was re-erected in 1779, the mound was excavated and a skeleton was found.

Valle Crucis Abbey

5. At a left bend in the lane, keep ahead to enter a caravan site and
    follow a track through the site. When it bends left continue
    ahead over grass between caravans. Cross a footbridge over the
    Eglwyseg River and take a path up the hillside. On reaching a
    footpath signpost, turn left. Cross a stile and walk beside the left
    edge of a long field to a ladder stile near a house. Turn right to
    another stile. Bear left on a track, and in 200 metres, turn right
    on another track, which is signposted Brynhyfryd.

6. Follow this lovely track through the woodlands to a stile at a
    gate. Cross another stile and continue on a track that descends
    with a fence on the right. Pass a house on the right and continue
    between fields to a lane. Turn right and ignore a lane on the left.
    Walk downhill and ignore a path into woodland. Immediately
    after the road crosses a stream, bear left over a stile signposted
    Castell Dinas Bran.

7. Follow the left boundary of the field to a gate. Do not go into the
    next field, but bear right. Follow a line of small trees on the left
    and walk uphill to a stile in the corner of the field. Cross and
    bear left to walk beside a fence. Keep left at a junction. The path
    undulates a little and follows a fence on the left, sometimes at a
    distance. From the path are fine views of the Eglwyseg cliffs.

8. Cross a stile and continue ahead between trees. Pass the corner
    of a field and walk uphill towards gorse. Join a path coming from
    a stile at the lane and follow the arrows. Bear right uphill to-
    wards the summit of Dinas Bran. On reaching a short wooden
    fence, turn right uphill to a stile. Go directly uphill and follow
    the waymarks to the ruins on top of the hill.

    The dramatic ruins of the castle crowning the summit of Dinas Bran are
    visible for many miles along the Vale of Llangollen. The medieval castle
    was built on the site of an Iron Age hill fort, which was traditionally be-
    lieved to have been founded by Bran. Other medieval stories suggest
    that this was the castle of the Holy Grail.

    The hill is a magnificent viewpoint with spectacular views of the Eglwyseg
    escarpment and the Vale of Llangollen. It is thought Gruffudd ap
    Madoc, a prince of Powys, built the stone castle about 1260. During Ed-
    ward I's campaign in Wales, Castell Dinas Bran was deliberately burnt
    and abandoned by its Welsh garrison to prevent use by the English.

When Henry de Lacy and his English army found it destroyed on 12 May 1277, he recommended that it be rebuilt. However, it is thought no repairs were carried out. The castle was given to the Earl of Surrey, who lived at Holt Castle.

9. Walk through the ruins to a footpath on the other side of the hill. The path zigzags downhill and gives superb views of the River Dee and Eglwyseg cliffs. After a final left bend, the path heads towards a house. Go through a kissing gate to the right of the house and follow the track ahead.

10. On reaching a junction, keep ahead on a track between hedges. At its end, go through a kissing gate on the right. Follow the left-hand fence downhill and pass a house. Join a tarmac path and emerge on a lane. Cross to a kissing gate and continue on a path. Pass a school on the right and descend some steps. Cross a bridge over the canal and bear right. Descend steps to a road and bear left to retrace your outward route into Llangollen.

19. Glyndyfrdwy to Carrog

Route: This short linear walk links the two Llangollen Railway stations of Glyndyfrdwy and Carrog in the beautiful Dee valley. Some climbing is necessary to cross the hillside between the two villages. There are lovely views along the way.

Distance: 3½ miles.

How to get there: Glyndyfrdwy is on the A5. Take the road to the station. Roadside parking nearby. Return by train from Carrog. Alternatively, park in Llangollen and take the train to Glyndyfrdwy.

Public Transport: Seasonal trains from Llangollen to Glyndyfrdwy and Carrog. Wrexham-Barmouth buses pass through Llangollen, Glyndyfrdwy and Llidiart y Parc, which is on the A5, 300 metres south of Carrog station.

Start: GR 151429. Glyndyfrdwy station (Llangollen Railway).

Finish:GR 118435.Carrog station (Llangollen Railway).

Maps: OS Landranger 125 or Pathfinder 805.

Located in the lovely Dee valley, the small villages of Glyndyfrdwy and Carrog have stations on the Llangollen Railway. This railway and the Bala Lake Railway are the only lines open on the former Ruabon to Barmouth (Morfa Mawddach) line. It opened in the 1860s but closed one hundred years later because it was no longer profitable. The line connected the north-west of England with the Cambrian coast line. There were thirty-one stopping places on the fifty-four mile line. The journey took three hours. Since the early 1980s, the Llangollen Railway Society has gradually opened the section of line that runs west from Llangollen.

The Tea Shop

On the scenic Llangollen Railway, Carrog station with its cosy Tea Room has been restored to its 1950s condition. The tea room menu includes pasties, cakes, scones and cream, bara brith and hot and cold drinks. Days and hours of opening fit in with the trains. It is usually open when the trains are running. The railway operates at

Easter and the following weekends. From late May trains run daily until the end of October. Tel: 01978 860951 (train times).

The Walk

1. From Glyndyfrdwy station, bear left and cross the bridge over the River Dee. On reaching a lane junction, turn left and ignore a lane on the right signposted Bryneglwys.

2. In another 200 metres cross a stile on the right and follow a fence uphill. Go through some bushes in front of a house and cross a stile. Bear left to another stile and walk downhill beside a fence on the left to a footbridge and stile. Bear slightly left uphill to a gap between bushes and a fence. Continue with a fence on the right and cross a stile beside a gate. Follow an enclosed path to a lane.

3. Turn right on the lane and in 500 metres you will pass a farm-house on the left. After another 300 metres, where the lane starts to descend, there is a field gate on the left. Ignore the gate but, in a few paces, go through the next gate onto a track.

Looking towards Llantysilio Mountain

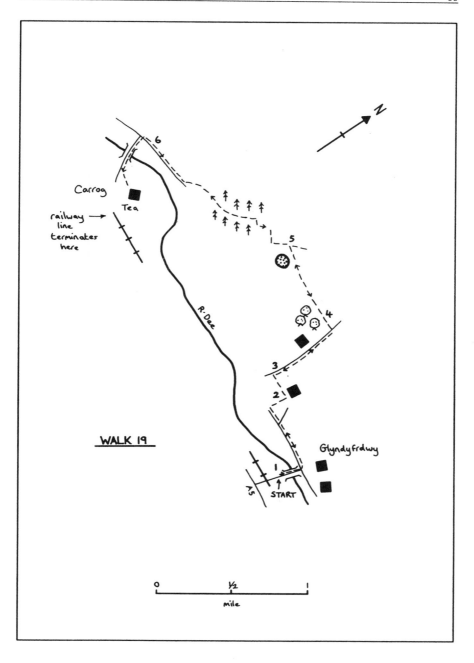

WALK 19

0   ½   1
mile

4. In a few metres, where the track divides, take the left-hand fork. It rises to pass trees on the left. Go through a gate and continue ahead on a clear path. There are views ahead of Llantysilio Mountain. Go through another gate and continue uphill to a stile beside a gate. Bear slightly right as you walk ahead and pass a pool on your left.

5. Cross a stile and bear half-left. There are now views of the Dee valley. Pass the length of a small quarry and follow a track towards coniferous trees. On reaching the edge of the forest, continue on the track with the forest on the left. In approximately 100 metres, cross a stile on the left. Walk downhill through the forest. When the track bends left, continue ahead on a narrow path. In about 100 metres, look for railed steps on the left. From this point there are beautiful views of the River Dee. Bear right to descend the hill to a stile near a gate. Turn right along the lane to Carrog.

    The original name of Carrog was Llansantffraid Glyndyfrdwy, meaning the Church of St Bridget in the valley of the Dee. The 12th-century church was destroyed by floods in 1601 and eleven years later a new church was built higher up the hill. A 14th-century house called Cachardy Owain was located in the village until demolished by the council. Owain Glyndwr had used the stone building as a prison. Glyndwr lived on the south side of the Dee. His house was situated 800 metres east of Llidiart y Parc near a mound called Owain Glyndwr's Mount. He had another estate at Sycharth in the Tanat valley.

    Glyndwr was a descendant of the Princes of Powys and Deheubarth. He trained as a soldier and studied law in London. Conflict arose when Lord Grey of Ruthin claimed a piece of common land to which Glyndwr had rights. In September 1400 Glyndwr and his supporters met at his house near Carrog and from there attacked Ruthin. His hope was for a free Wales. During the first few year of his war, his army increased and he won many battles throughout Wales. In 1404 he captured Harlech Castle and summoned his first Parliament at Machynlleth. A year later the tide began to turn against him. In 1409 the English won back the castle and Glyndwr's family were taken as prisoners to London. Owain Glyndwr avoided capture and it is thought he died in Herefordshire in September 1415.

6. Bear left to cross the bridge over the River Dee. Follow the lane to Carrog station and tea room.

20. Corwen

Route: This interesting walk climbs through woodland to a fine viewpoint before crossing the Dee valley to an Iron Age hill fort. Most of the route is along tracks and lanes.

Distance: 6¼ miles.

How to get there: Corwen is on the A5, west of Llangollen.

Public Transport: Buses from Barmouth, Wrexham, Llangollen and Ruthin.

Start: GR 079434. Corwen Square. Car park nearby.

Maps: OS Landranger 125 or OS Pathfinder 805.

The Tea Shop

Situated on the A5, Corwen Manor is a fascinating craft shop and café. The building was erected in the 19th century to house paupers from the surrounding parishes. Since then it has been used as a factory, but later became dilapidated. The Orissor Trust took it over in 1981 and carried out extensive repairs. Nine years later the Sayers family bought the building and gave it the name Corwen Manor. The craft shop is stocked with many interesting items and there is a candle workshop. Bed and breakfast is also available. The café menu includes soup, toasties, sandwiches and scones with cream. Open every day from May to September. Hours Monday to Saturday 10.15am-5.00pm. Sundays 11.30am-5.00pm. During the rest of the year it is closed on Tuesdays, Wednesdays and Thursdays and on the other days it is open 11.30am-4.00pm. Tel: 01490 413196.

The Walk

1. In the square walk towards the NatWest bank and pass the Owain Glyndwr Hotel on the left. Immediately bear left to walk towards the back of the hotel. Go through the church lychgate.

    Corwen Church is dedicated to St Mael and St Sulien, who came as missionaries in the sixth century. Near the lychgate are some late 18th-century low gravestones, which have places to kneel on them. In the churchyard, near the south-west corner of the church, stands the medieval shaft of a cross which is similar in design to Eliseg's Pillar near Llangollen. It is set in a stone which has small depressions in it and these may be cup marks. These marks appear on stones in England and Wales, but very few are known in Wales. On a stone forming a lintel above the south door there is a mark reputed to be made by Owain Glyndwr's dagger. During a fit of rage, he flung it from Pen y Pigyn, the hill behind the church. The stone was probably a Celtic cross. Many changes and additions have been made to the church, which was begun in the 13th century. It has a Norman font.

The medieval cross in Corwen churchyard

2. When ready to leave the churchyard, face the church at the north door and turn right to follow a path to a turn stile gate. Turn left on the lane. When the road surface ends, continue on a path. Ignore a wide path that joins from the left and continue ahead to a fork. On the right is a Druid's Circle (Gorsedd) that was built for the 1919 National Victory Eisteddfod held in Corwen. Bear left uphill through the forest and, shortly, follow an old wall on the right. The path descends to a footbridge and in approximately another 60 metres emerges at the viewpoint and monument.

From Pen y Pigyn are fine views of the Dee valley, Caer Drewyn hill fort and Corwen. The monument was erected to commemorate the marriage of the Prince of Wales (King Edward VII) with Princess Alexandra of Denmark on 10 March 1863. It was restored to commemorate the investi-

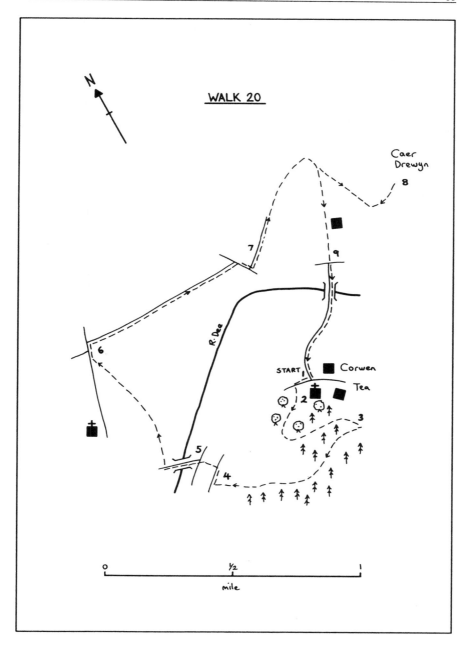

ture at Caernarfon of the Prince of Wales in 1911. This is the spot from which Owain Glyndwr is said to have hurled his dagger.

3. From the back of the monument take a path that leads to a forest track. Turn right to a gate and stile. On reaching another track, turn right downhill. In approximately 600 metres, turn right on a narrower track. Go through a gate and pass a reservoir and a house on the right. Follow a fence bordering the forest on the left and go through a small gate. Walk downhill on an old walled path and ignore a path on the right. Go through a small gate and, shortly, reach a road.

4. Turn right and in approximately 150 metres turn left on a path. Go down some steps and ignore a path on the right. Continue down the steps to emerge at the road junction of the A5 and B4401.

5. Turn left on the A5 in the direction of Betws y Coed. Cross the bridge over the River Dee and ignore a stile on the right. Continue a few metres and turn right on a lane. It soon becomes a grassy, hedged track. In 800 metres join a track coming from a house and bear left to the A494.

    Rug Chapel is 400 metres to the left downhill on the A494. It was built in the 17th century for Colonel William Salusbury, who was known as 'Old Blue Stocking'. A Royalist, he defended Denbigh Castle for three years in the Civil War. The highly decorated chapel contains carvings of animals and a wall painting of a reclining skeleton.

6. At the end of the track, turn right on the A494 and in 150 metres, bear right on a lane. Follow it until you join a road near a bend. At this point there are fine views of the River Dee and Corwen. Cross the road and turn right. Shortly, turn left on another lane.

7. The lane crosses the Corwen Cutting and passes the track to Trewyn Bach. Continue on the lane downhill to where it becomes a track and forks. Bear right uphill and ignore another track going through a gate on the left. Walk uphill and take another track on the right at a signpost to Caer Drewyn hill fort. Cross a stile and bear left on a track that slants to the right uphill. As you climb you will have good views across the Dee valley.

When the track starts to descend, look for a break in the bank on your left.

Caer Drewyn Iron Age hill fort is in an impressive position overlooking the Dee valley. The rampart encircling the crest of the hill is about 800 metres in length. The entrance is through the small enclosure on the north-east side of the hill, near the track. The fort was probably used as headquarters in 1165 by Owain Gwynedd before his battle with Henry II.

8. After your explorations, retrace your steps to the track at the bottom of the hill. Turn left and follow the grassy track to a stile. Pass a farmhouse on the left and continue on the track to a road.

9. Bear right and in 50 metres turn left to cross the River Dee. Follow the road into Corwen. On reaching the square, turn left and you will shortly see Corwen Manor on your right.

21. Trevor

Route: River, canal, woodland and hillside paths are combined on this lovely walk, which features a country park with farm animals and the crossing of the breath-taking Pontcysyllte aqueduct. The route includes some pavement walking.

Distance: 5¼ miles.

How to get there: Leave the A5 at Froncysyllte to take the B5434 towards Trevor. In one mile, on reaching the canal, turn right to the car park. Alternatively, follow the A539 to Trevor.

Public Transport: Buses from Wrexham and Llangollen to Trevor.

Start: GR 272423. Car park at Trevor wharf.

Maps: OS Landranger 117 or OS Pathfinder 806.

Trevor wharf is located at the northern end of the Pontcysyllte aqueduct on the Shropshire Union Canal. From here narrow boats leave the basin to cross 'the sky'. The canal and aqueduct were built to provide a link between the Severn and the Dee, but the north-east extension to Wrexham and Chester was never completed. Nowadays, the branch waterway going west to Llangollen is very popular with pleasure craft. It ends at Llantysilio near the man-made Horseshoe Falls, which supplies water to the canal.

The Tea Shop

There are two possibilities.

On the route, **Cliff's Café** in Froncysyllte is not exactly a tea shop, but it is a popular stop for walkers seeking refreshments. Hot meals including soup, sandwiches, scones and hot and cold drinks are on offer. Open all year every day 8.00am until 6.00pm. On Saturdays it closes at 4.00pm. Tel: 01691 774684.

At the end of the walk, and close to the canal, is the **Trevor Wharf Canal Gift Shop**. Soup, hot and cold drinks and biscuits are served. There are tables outside. Open all year. Summer opening hours are 8.30am until 5.00pm. Winter hours are 11.00am to 4.00pm.

Pontcysyllte aqueduct

The Walk

1. From the car park walk out to the canal and turn left. Pass the footbridge on your right and turn left at a footpath signpost. Ignore a stile on the left and descend to a level area below the Pontcysyllte aqueduct. Descend the steps on your left to the River Dee.

2. Turn left on the path and follow it to a track near a building. Cross a footbridge over a stream and bear right to continue on a path close to the river. Go up some steps and emerge at paddocks in Ty Mawr Country Park.

    Ty Mawr is an unspoilt area of grassland, rich in wild flowers. A number of donkeys, ponies, rare breeds of sheep, hens and ducks are kept here. Bags of food to feed them can be bought in the Visitor Centre. The country park holds a number of events for children during the year and a leaflet listing them is obtainable from the centre and tourist offices. There are picnic tables in the park and cold drinks are on sale. The centre is usually open every day from April to September and at weekends from October to March.

3.   Turn left and, shortly, bear right between the paddocks. Go through a kissing gate into a field. From this point there is a fine view of Cefn viaduct.

The Cefn viaduct carries the Chester to Shrewsbury railway line. Built in 1848 by Henry Robertson, it stands 147 feet high and each of its 19 arches spans 60 feet.

4.   Turn left over a stile to the Visitors Centre. Walk ahead to a road and turn right. The road bends to the left and goes under a bridge. On reaching the B5065, turn right and follow the pavement. Pass the village of Pentre and ignore a footpath on the right. Cross the canal and, almost immediately, climb over a stile on the right.

5.   With the canal below on the right, walk ahead through the field. You are now following a section of the Offa's Dyke Path. Pass some trees at an old field boundary and continue to a stile. Cross the dyke and turn left over another stile. Walk ahead beside the dyke to the A5.

6.   Turn right, and in approximately 40 metres cross the road to a metal bar stile in a wall. Follow the left boundary of a field to a corner stile. Cross the next field diagonally right to the top corner. Go through a gap into another field and bear left to a stile and lane.

7.   At this point the walk leaves the Offa's Dyke Path. Cross the lane and walk uphill on a track. In 500 metres, where the track bends left, turn right to cross a stile. Walk towards some trees, with fine views to your right, and pass a small wood on your left. When the wood ends, keep ahead and cross a stile on the left.

8.   Bear right and head downhill towards some protruding woodland. Pass the wood on your right and follow an old field boundary on your right to a stile. Descend a steep path through woodlands to a stony path. Turn right and follow the main path. Continue to an open space directly above the A5. Look on your left for a hidden path and follow it downhill to the road. Turn left and in about 40 metres, Cliff's Café is on your right.

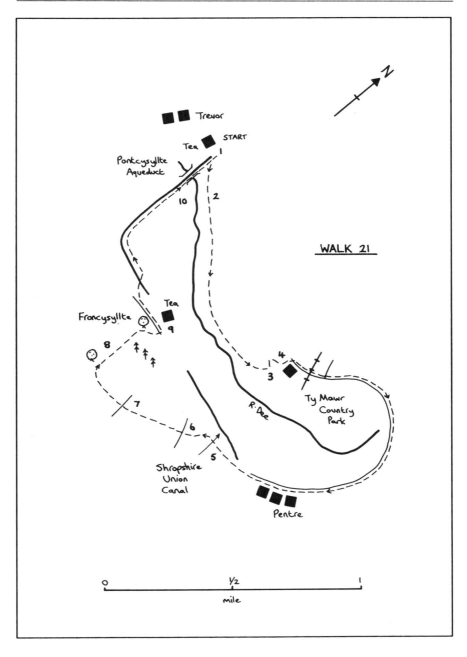

Trevor

Tea START

Pontcysyllte
Aqueduct

10 2

WALK 21

Tea

Froncysyllte 9

8

Ty Mawr
Country
Park

4
3

7

R. Dee

6

5

Shropshire
Union
Canal

Pentre

0 ½ 1
mile

9. Continue beside the A5 and pass the traffic lights in Froncysyllte. In another 150 metres, take a road on your right signposted Trevor. Immediately bear right on a lane which shortly swings to the left and descends to the canal. Cross the footbridge and turn left. Go through a wooden kissing gate and follow the towpath to the Pontcysyllte aqueduct.

Taking ten years to build, the Pontcysyllte aqueduct was completed in 1805 at a cost of £47,018. The work of Thomas Telford, it has 18 stone piers, some of which stand 126 feet above the River Dee. The canal is carried 1007 feet in a cast iron trough. The iron is said to be jointed with Welsh flannel and lead that have been dipped in boiling sugar, whilst the mortar between the stones of the piers contain ox blood and lime. The opening ceremony in November 1805 was attended by a flotilla of boats and a huge crowd. A narrow towpath with railings runs alongside the trough.

10. Cross the aqueduct above the River Dee. Trevor Wharf Canal Gift Shop is on the opposite side of the footbridge.

22. Erddig

Route: This is an easy, lovely walk through meadows and woodlands in Erddig Country Park. There is one short climb.

Distance: 3½ miles.

How to get there: Erddig is off the A5152, south of Wrexham, and is well signposted.

Public Transport: The nearest bus stop is at Felin Puleston, which is on the Wrexham-Llangollen and Wrexham-Oswestry bus routes.

Start: GR 328482. Car park at Erddig house.

Maps: OS Landranger 117 or OS Pathfinder 806.

Erddig house dates from the late 17th century. The original owner ran into debt and it was sold to John Meller who added two wings and laid out the gardens. His nephew, Simon Yorke, inherited the estate in 1733 and it remained with the Yorke family until it was given to the National Trust in 1973. Completely unmodernised, the house had suffered years of neglect, and also subsidence from coal being mined under the house. The house and gardens have gradually been restored. Because nothing was ever thrown away by the Yorkes, the house is full of fascinating collections, from portraits of servants to antique furniture and vintage cars.

The Tea Shop

Erddig Restaurant is in the old country house now owned by the National Trust. Many of the dishes on offer are based on Georgian and Welsh recipes. Morning coffee, lunches and afternoon teas are served. The extensive menu includes home-made soups, savoury tarts, Welsh cream tea, plum cake and parkin. There is a good selection of drinks including speciality teas and traditional home-made lemonade. Non NT members will need to pay the normal admission fee to the property. Open April to October 11.00am-5.15pm. Closed on Thursdays and Fridays. Tel: 01978 355314.

The Walk

1. From the car park, walk out of the exit and follow the drive. Go through a kissing gate near a cattle grid and pass the dovecote on your left. Pass the entrance to the car park and, at a fork in the drive, keep ahead to follow a railing on the right. In about 60 metres, bear right on a track signposted Cup and Saucer Waterfall. Walk downhill and in approximately 400 metres you will see a footbridge on your left leading to the waterfall.

    The ornamental cup and saucer waterfall is a weir that was built in 1774. It feeds the hydraulic ram pump which elevates some of the water to a greater height in Erddig gardens.

The cup and saucer waterfall

Opposite the waterfall is a kissing gate which gives access to Big Wood and a 12th-century motte and bailey castle. The path follows a section of the 8th-century Wat's Dyke, which ran from near Holywell to Maesbury.

2. Return to the track and continue along it. Cross a bridge and follow the track to the next bridge. In about another 120 metres,

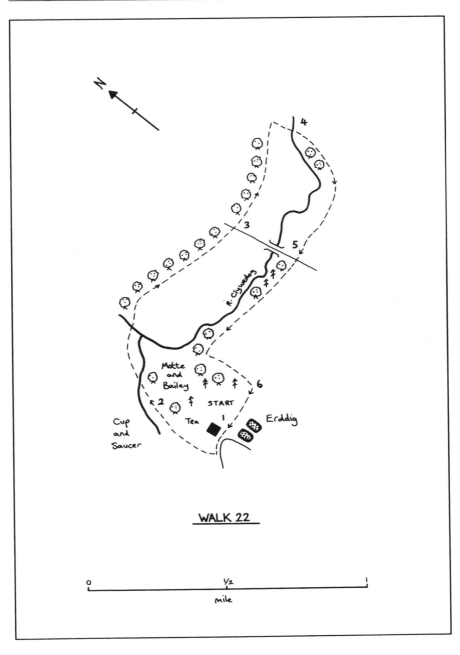

WALK 22

turn right through a kissing gate into Coed y Glyn wood. Follow the path along the edge of the woodland to a kissing gate and lane.

3. Turn right to go through a kissing gate on the opposite side of the lane. The path continues through more woodland and in approximately 700 metres it descends to a stile. Bear left through the field to have the wood on your left. Pass through a gap in the hedge to another field and, in a few metres, bear right to a lower path. Turn right and follow it to a footbridge over the River Clywedog.

4. After crossing the bridge, bear right on a waymarked path to walk above the river. Go through some woodland and descend steps to cross a footbridge. Cross a stile and follow a fence on the right to a corner. Go up to a waymarked post and continue uphill. You will pass a couple of isolated trees and another waymark. Walk along the right side of the field to a stile.

5. Turn left along the lane and, in approximately 40 metres, turn right through a kissing gate. Follow a fence on your left along the edge of a wood. Ignore other paths and continue ahead with fields on the left. In about 800 metres the path enters woodland. Bear left at a junction, and return to the edge of the wood to have the field again on your left. You will shortly see Erddig house and gardens on your right.

6. Go through a kissing gate into a field and turn right. Walk through the field to another kissing gate. You will see the dovecote ahead, and will shortly emerge on the drive at Erddig.

23. Erbistock

Route: A short walk beside a very beautiful stretch of the River Dee. Some of the woodland paths may be muddy and slippery after wet weather.

Distance: 3½ miles.

How to get there: Leave the A528 at Overton Bridge, ½ mile south of its junction with the A539. Take a minor road in the direction of Erbistock for about 1 mile to The Garden House Plant Centre.

Public Transport: Infrequent buses from Wrexham to Overton Bridge, ½ mile from point 6.

Start: GR 354415. The Garden House Plant Centre, Erbistock. Walkers visiting the tea room can leave their cars in the car park at the market garden.

Maps: OS Landranger 117 or OS Pathfinder 806.

The Tea Shop

The Garden House Plant Centre is in a lovely position above the River Dee. Seasonal organic vegetables, soft fruit, cut flowers, herbs and honey are on sale. The tea room serves coffee, tea, cold drinks and home-made cakes. Open from 31 March until 31 October. Open on weekdays 10.00am-5.00pm, Saturdays 11.00am-5.00pm, Sundays 2.00pm-5.00pm. Tel: 01978 780958.

The Walk

1. From the car park at the market garden, turn right on the lane and in a few metres turn right through a small gate. Keep ahead and at the end of the garden cross a track to a gate. Follow a path downhill into St Hilary's churchyard.

    St Hilary's Church is a neat 19th-century sandstone building on the northern bank of the River Dee. Erbistock is an ancient settlement and the first church was dedicated to St Erbin, a Celtic saint. It is thought the Normans changed the dedication to St Hilary. Near the south porch there is a sundial dated 1702.

2.   Bear right to a gate and lane. Turn right for a few metres then bear left down steps. Pass the old ferry's winch on your left.

A small ferry boat used to carry passengers across the River Dee at Erbistock until the late 1930s. It was attached to ropes spanning the river and the winch that used to pull the ferry to and fro still stands. The 17th-century inn is built of local sandstone. Look out for mallard, moorhen, dipper and grey wagtail on this walk.

3.   Walk ahead below a wall and the Boat Inn to a stile. Continue with the River Dee on your left through a field. Cross a stile into woodland and follow the riverside path, which passes short stretches of red sandstone cliffs. Cross a plank bridge and emerge out of the trees to follow a fence. Continue on the path through another stretch of woodland. After crossing a stream go up to a stile and enter a field.

The River Dee near Erbistock

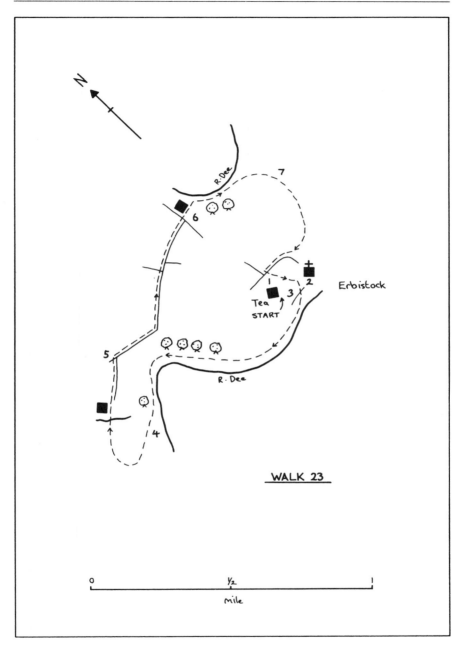

R. Dee

7

6

Erbistock

Tea
START

1
2
3

5

R. Dee

4

WALK 23

0
½
1

mile

4. Leave the river by bearing right into another field. Follow a hedge on your left in the direction of a farm. At a gate turn right to continue with a fence on the left. Before reaching the end of the field, bear slightly right to a stile next to a gate. Bear left on a track and cross a ford. Join an access lane and pass a house on the left. Walk uphill to a lane junction.

5. Turn right and take the next lane on the left. Walk downhill and ignore a lane on the left and one on the right. At the next junction, cross the road directly to a stile.

6. Descend a path through the trees to the River Dee close to Erbistock Mill. Bear right to follow a path above the river. After rain the path may be slippery and in places it is necessary to stride over fallen tree trunks. In about 500 metres the path leaves the wood and crosses a field to a stile and track.

7. Cross the stile almost opposite and bear slightly right to walk below a hill. Continue with a hedge on the right. When the hedge veers right, walk ahead. Bear slightly left to go through a gap into the next field. Follow a hedge on your right and cross a stile near a gate. Turn right to walk beside a high wall and a hedge. Emerge on a lane and turn right to the market garden and the start of the walk.

24. Chirk

Route: A superb, varied walk with many interesting features. Riverside paths are followed by a section of the Offa's Dyke Path, and an optional visit to Chirk Castle. The return to Chirk goes along the Shropshire Union Canal towpath, which passes through two long tunnels. A torch may be useful.

Distance: 8 miles.

How to get there: Chirk is off the A5, north of Oswestry.

Public Transport: Buses from Oswestry, Wrexham and Llangollen. Trains on the Chester-Shrewsbury line stop at Chirk.

Start: GR 291378. Chirk car park.

Maps: OS Landrangers 117 and 126 or OS Pathfinders 806 and 827.

The Normans built a castle at Chirk and another nearby across the English border. It is thought the town's name may be derived from the River Ceiriog. The church dates from the 15th century and holds monuments to the Myddleton family of Chirk Castle.

The Tea Shop

There are two possible refreshment stops.

In the summer months you have the option of visiting **Chirk Castle** and taking refreshments in the Tea Room. The varied menu includes hot dishes, home-made soup, flans, salads, savoury scones and a selection of home-made cakes. Non National Trust members will have to pay an admission fee. Open Easter until the end of September Wednesday to Sunday. Closed on Mondays and Tuesdays apart from Bank Holiday Mondays. In October it is open only on Saturdays and Sundays. Hours throughout the season are 12 noon until 5.00pm. Tel: 01691 777701.

The **Snack Bar** in Chirk serves hot and cold drinks, snacks and cakes. Open all year Monday-Saturday 9.00am-6.00pm. Sundays 11.00am-5.00pm.

The Walk

1. From the car park, walk out to the main road and turn left. Pass the traffic lights and the church. When the road curves to the right downhill, continue along the pavement. In 60 metres look for a gap in the hedge on the left and climb over the fence type stile. Walk downhill on a clear path towards some houses. Bear left on an embankment to follow a line of trees on your right. Cross a wooden fence and in 20 metres leave the embankment to pass buildings on the left. Join a track coming from the former mill and walk up to the road.

2. Cross the road to the stile opposite. Follow a track downhill to a field and continue ahead to follow the River Ceiriog on your left. Cross a stile under the aqueduct and another below the railway viaduct. Continue beside the river. Keep a look out for herons. Leave the field by crossing a stile near a gate. Turn left over Pont-faen bridge into Shropshire. Immediately turn right along a narrow lane. In 100 metres, where the lane starts to go uphill, cross a stile on the right.

    You are now on the Maelor Way, a walk that links the Sandstone Trail and Shropshire Way with the Offa's Dyke Path.

3. Walk ahead to follow a track beside the river into another field. Go through a gap into a long field and continue ahead. Cross a stile into Pentre Wood and ignore a path on the left. Keep the river on your right. Cross a small footbridge and walk uphill, shortly going up steps. The pools of Chirk fishery are in view below. After descending a few steps, turn left. Cross a stile and bear left to have views of Chirk Castle on your right. Cross a stile and continue on an enclosed track. Go through three gates and follow the track to a lane.

4. Turn right and follow the lane downhill. Pass some lime kilns on the left and bear right down a steep lane. You are now on the Offa's Dyke Path. Cross the River Ceiriog to emerge on the B4500 in Wales.

    It is thought that the Battle of Crogen took place hereabouts near a break in Offa's Dyke. In 1165 advance soldiers of Henry II's army were defeated by the Welsh troops of Owain Gwynedd. After suffering heavy

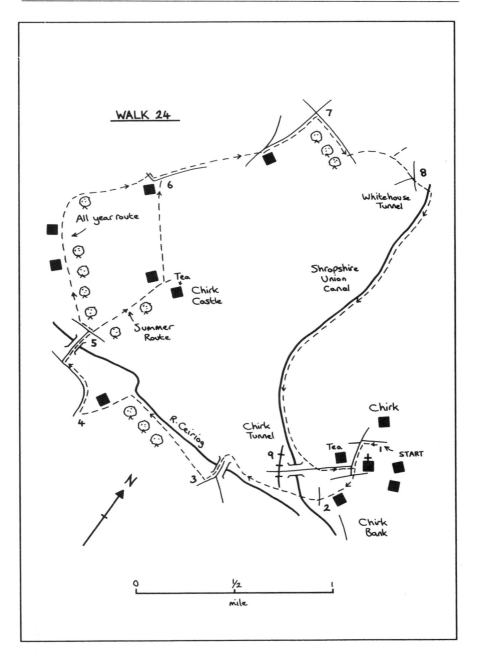

WALK 24

All year route

Whitehouse
Tunnel

Shropshire
Union
Canal

Tea
Chirk
Castle

Summer
Route

R. Ceiriog

Chirk
Tunnel

Chirk

Tea

START

Chirk
Bank

N

0   ½   1
        mile

losses, the king was forced to retreat and the English dead were buried in the dyke. Further west, on the Berwyn moorland, there is a track known as Ffordd Saeson, the Englishman's Road, from when King Henry and his army retreated along it.

5.   You now have a choice of routes. If you wish to visit Chirk Castle, follow the summer route, which is open to walkers 1 April-30 September.
     Summer route: Cross the road and bear slightly right through a stone arch and follow a path through the wood. It shortly goes uphill and crosses the dyke. After crossing a stile, walk up the field to a stile and woodland. Follow the path to a track and turn left. At a track junction, turn right. on reaching a fork, bear left to the castle.

The Ceiriog Valley from the Offa's Dyke Path

Chirk Castle has been occupied almost continuously as a castle and stately home for about 700 years. The building dates from the 13th century when Roger Mortimer was given the area by Edward I. There have been many alterations since then. Sir Thomas Myddleton purchased the castle for about £5000 in 1595 and he added another range. His

son was a Parliamentarian and he lost the castle to the Royalists during the Civil War. They held it for three years until the Myddletons regained the castle and changed allegiance. In revenge the
Parliamentarians besieged the castle in 1659 and destroyed part of it.
After the Restoration a new east range was added. Although the
Myddleton family live in part of the building, it is now in the care of the
National Trust. Visitors to the castle can see the elegant furniture and
fine tapestries and paintings. Do not miss the dungeon or the beautiful
formal gardens.

Continuation of summer route. After visiting the castle, return
to the junction and walk ahead to the stables. There are picnic
tables here. Turn left and cross a stile. Follow the track to a lane
and turn right to join the all-year route.

All-year route: Cross the road and bear left uphill on a narrow
lane. Ignore a track on the left and keep ahead. On reaching a
fork near a house, bear right to pass the house on your left. Continue uphill to reach Crogenwladys Farm. Pass the buildings on
your left and walk uphill on a rough track beside woodland.
When the track levels, look for a stile on the right. Walk uphill
through a field to a gate. Views open up ahead and, as you descend, Chirk Castle can be seen across fields to your right. Continue over stiles and follow a track towards a house. Cross a stile
to the left of the house and turn right along the lane.

6. Now with the all year and summer route rejoined on the Offa's
    Dyke Path, follow the lane for approximately 600 metres. When
    the lane starts to descend, cross a stile on the left and bear right
    to another stile. Continue ahead on a visible path some distance
    from the right-hand fence. Cross a stile near a gate and follow a
    track to a lane. Turn left and at a junction take the right-hand
    fork downhill. Pass a cottage on the right and reach a crossroads.

7. Turn right, leaving the Offa's Dyke Path. Pass some woodland
    and, when the lane bends sharp right, turn left over a fence type
    stile next to a gate. Follow the right-hand fence for a few metres,
    then slant to the right and pass an isolated tree on your right.
    Cross a stile at the bottom of the field and follow an enclosed
    path to a bend. Ignore the path ahead and bear right to continue
    on the enclosed path to a stile. Walk downhill and go through a

gap into the next field. Bear left beside a hedge and walk uphill to a stile at a gate. Turn left along the lane to the A5.

8. Cross the road with care and turn right. In 50 metres turn left through a gap in some trees and follow a path to the Shropshire union Canal. Turn left through the 174 metre Whitehouse tunnel. There is a handrail, and a bench on the other side. Continue on the towpath for 1½ miles to the Chirk tunnel. It emerges at the aqueduct, which is alongside the railway viaduct.

The 421 metre Chirk tunnel was constructed so that the view from the castle would not be spoilt by the canal and its traffic. On the southern side of the tunnel is the Chirk aqueduct. Although not as impressive as the Pontcysyllte aqueduct, it is nevertheless an impressive structure, standing 70 feet above the River Ceiriog. Built by Thomas Telford between 1796 and 1801, it carries the canal from Wales to England and is supported by ten arches. Beside it is the taller 19th-century viaduct of the Shrewsbury-Chester railway line.

Before returning to Chirk, you may like to cross the aqueduct and follow the towpath to Chirk Bank. The Post Office on the opposite side of the road serves tea and snacks, but there is no seating apart from a bench near the canal.

9. From the tunnel, walk up to the road. Cross to the pavement and bear right to follow it into Chirk. At the junction, turn left to the start and car park.

25. Glyn Ceiriog

Route: A varied walk which includes a riverside track and a gradual climb out of the valley. There are splendid views along the way.

Distance: 6¼ miles.

How to get there: Glyn Ceiriog is on the B4500, west of Chirk.

Public Transport: Buses from Llangollen, Chirk and Oswestry.

Start: GR 201377. Signposted car park near the Glyn Valley Hotel.

Maps: OS Landranger 125 and 126 or OS Pathfinders 826 and 827.

The Tea Shop

The Ceiriog Christian Centre extends a welcome to all who visit the centre for a chat or to buy light refreshments. All work done by the interdenominational centre is voluntary. Greeting cards, Christian books in English and Welsh, and crafts from Third World Countries are on sale. Snacks on offer are very reasonably priced and include soup, sandwiches, beans on toast, scones and cakes. The centre is near the crossroads in the village of Glyn Ceiriog, on the road to Chirk. Open on Mondays, Tuesdays, Thursdays and Fridays 10.30am-3.30pm. Saturdays 10.30am-12.30pm. Tel: 01691 718609.

The Walk

1. From the car park, walk out onto the B4500 and turn right. After passing the Ddol Hir caravan site on the left, look for a track on the left. It leads to a stile and the Glyn Valley Tramway.

    The Glyn Valley Tramway first opened in 1873 to carry slate from Glyn Ceiriog to Chirk. The horse-drawn tramway ran beside the road through the valley to Pontfaen bridge. From the bridge there was a steep gradient for 800 metres and the wagons had to be uncoupled before being pulled out of the valley to the Shropshire Union Canal. Although the tramway carried 4000 tons of slate each year and passengers, it was not profitable, mainly because of the extra horses needed to pull the wagons from Pontfaen. After 1878, when the Hendre quarries opened,

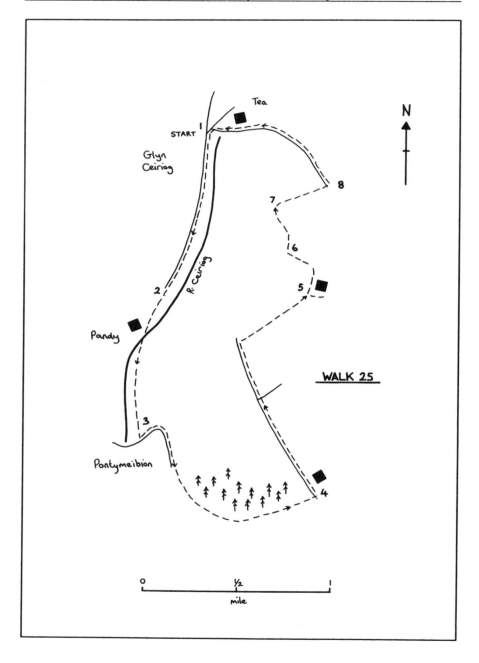

the tramway company extended the line to a total of nine miles. They converted to steam and re-routed the line to Chirk station. Locomotives were not allowed to travel at more than ten miles per hour. From 1891 to 1933 the company ran a passenger service with two trips each way per day. At its peak the company operated four locomotives, more than 250 wagons and 14 passenger coaches. Eventually road transport took over and the tramway closed in 1935. From the road to Pontymeibion the track is owned by the National Trust.

2. The path descends to follow the River Ceiriog. On reaching houses at Pandy, continue ahead and cross a bridge over the river. The track continues through woodland with the river on the right. Ignore a footpath on the left and follow the track to a lane near Pontymeibion.

The tramway ended 500 metres further on at the Hendre quarries. They were worked from 1875 to 1950 and produced stone for roads. George Borrow walked to Pontymeibion in 1854 whist visiting the birthplace of Huw Morris, a royalist and poet.

The Ceiriog Valley near Pandy

3. Turn left along the lane. After passing a house on the left, go through a gate across the lane. On your right are fine views of the valley. At a cattle grid go through a gate and continue on a track alongside the forest. Stay on the main track and, on reaching a fork, take the left-hand track. It is fairly level and later rejoins the other track. Continue with the forest on the left and go through a gate. When the forest ends, follow the track as it bends left to a lane.

4. Turn left along the lane and ignore another lane on the right. In another 500 metres, turn right on a bridleway. Walk beside a fence on your right and go through a gate onto an enclosed track. Follow it to a barn.

5. In front of the barn, turn left on a track, and in a few metres, where the track turns left through a gate, go ahead to cross a stile. Follow the right side of the field and cross into a higher field. Walk uphill to reach a line of gorse. Bear left to walk below the bushes. Enter another field and continue beside the fence to a stile.

6. Walk ahead, bearing slightly right, but be careful not to go far uphill. In about 150 metres, cross a broken wall. After another 100 metres you should pass the end of a wall on your right. In 50 metres you will reach the end of a hedge. Cross a wall and walk downhill with the hedge on your right until you meet a fence.

7. Bear right and follow a walled grassy track. Below on your left is Glyn Ceiriog. Walk downhill and, after crossing a couple of stiles, you will emerge in a field. Follow a fence on the right and cross a stile in a corner. Continue with the fence on your left to the next stile and some steps.

8. On reaching the lane, turn left and follow it to Glyn Ceiriog.

Tea Shop Walks – Spreading everywhere!

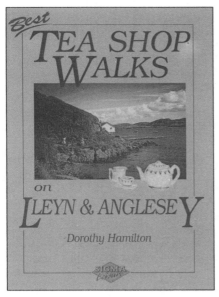

The Sigma Leisure Tea Shop Walks series already includes:

Cheshire

The Chilterns

The Cotswolds

The Lake District, Volume 1

The Lake District, Volume 2

Lancashire

Leicestershire & Rutland

The Lleyn Peninsula & Anglesey

North Devon

The Peak District

Shropshire

Snowdonia

South Devon

Staffordshire

Surrey & Sussex

Warwickshire

The Yorkshire Dales

Each book costs £6.95 and contains an average of 25 excellent walks: far better value than any other competitor!

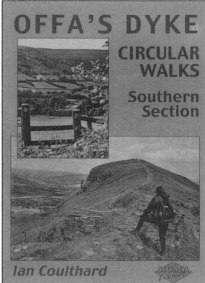

DISCOVERY WALKS IN NORTH WALES
Anna & Graham Francis
21 routes to sites of particular beauty or interest, from leisurely strolls of a couple of miles to more arduous 8-mile rambles. The book explores imposing castles, spectacular waterfalls, copper mines and steam railways. Anna Francis provides pen and ink drawings and there is also an aerial picture map for each route. £6.95

OFFA'S DYKE CIRCULAR WALKS (Two volumes - Northern and Southern Sections)
Ian Coulthard
Each book contains 25 energetic and challenging circular hill walks based on Offa's Dyke National Trail. Walks range from 5 to 13 miles (3 to 7 hours), and concise instructions include height gain, local facilities and summaries of terrain and ground conditions. Sketch maps are to scale – a boon in this demanding terrain. Suggested starting points give the more demanding elements in the first few miles. £7.95 per volume

In case of difficulty, or for a free catalogue, please contact:
SIGMA LEISURE, 1 SOUTH OAK LANE, WILMSLOW, CHESHIRE SK9 6AR.
Phone: 01625-531035
Fax: 01625-536800.
E-mail: info@sigmapress.co.uk
Web site: http//www.sigmapress.co.uk

VISA and MASTERCARD orders welcome.